VINTAGE ROSES

VINTAGE ROSES

beautiful varieties for home and garden

JANE EASTOE

photography by

GEORGIANNA LANE

GIBBS SMITH
TO ENRICH AND INSPIRE HUMANKIND

Contents

INTRODUCTION

OLDER THAN WE ARE BUT YOUNGER THAN THE DINOSAURS, THE ROSE HAS BEEN LINKED WITH HUMAN BEINGS ACROSS MANY MILLENNIA. IT HAS INSPIRED ARTISTS, SCULPTORS, WRITERS AND POETS, AND IS THE SUBJECT OF MYTH AND LEGEND. THE ROSE CAN HINT AT POLITICAL AFFILIATION, SPORTING LOYALTY, NATIONAL PRIDE, BEAUTY, VIRTUE, ROMANTIC YEARNING, LOVE, SEX AND SECRECY, AND IT IS ALSO HEAVY WITH RELIGIOUS SYMBOLISM. FAMOUS AS A FRAGRANCE, USED AS A CULINARY FLAVORING AND A SOURCE OF VITAMIN C, AND BELIEVED TO HAVE MEDICINAL AND THERAPEUTIC PROPERTIES, THE ROSE IS ONE OF OUR OLDEST CULTIVATED FLOWERS.

There are around 150 species of wild rose. These modest, five-petaled flowers are the fecund species that grow true from seed, content to reproduce merrily as nature intended. All other types of rose, of which there are literally thousands upon thousands of varieties, have been propagated, both accidentally and by design, to create exceptional flowers with a beauty of form and an intoxicatingly lovely fragrance.

This human meddling has created a bewildering array of Old and Modern rose classes, all subject to intense horticultural scrutiny. The characteristics, growth patterns, care and pruning regimes of the poetically named Damasks and Bourbons, the China and Tea roses, the Centifolias and the Portlands, the Floribundas and the Polyanthas, have all been helpfully and lovingly detailed. The sheer weight of information might lead you to believe that rose growing is a devilish business requiring a level of commitment akin to raising a child. Not so. It couldn't be simpler.

Arguably one of the hardest tasks in growing a rose is selecting the ideal one for your situation from the thousands that are on offer. There are fashions in roses, as in everything else, and our quest for perfection has taken us in some extravagant and colorful directions. The focus in this book is on the classic, ageless and enduring flowers, which we have dubbed Vintage roses.

This user-friendly term encompasses both the true Old roses and the best of the Modern roses. All Vintage roses have one thing in common: they are garden-friendly roses that celebrate the style and grace of the old. They are willing to integrate in mixed borders, to clothe walls, fences, pillars and pergolas, and to ramble picturesquely over the unsightly, without dominating or showing off. The modern Vintage rose salutes the Old rose, while improving on its form and fragrance, and adding an ability to repeat-flower as well as resistance to disease. Both Vintage roses and Old roses have seductive qualities, and they all produce graceful, generous, fragrant and accommodating flowers. As these glorious pictures by photographer Georgianna Lane illustrate, they are simply bewitching; a delight to both the eye and the nose.

So much has been written about the

Opposite François Debreuil (see p. 98)

technicalities of rose growing that it is easy to forget that, in their vintage form, roses are user-friendly garden plants, easy to grow and easy to look after. So let's dispel the notion that roses are hard work and require high levels of expertise. Many will settle for a light annual prune – it's not rocket science, just cut them back a bit – and ideally give them some annual feed.

I should own up that for me, growing roses is all about creating a cheap supply of fabulous, fragrant blooms. I'm no Martha Stewart; I just love cutting flowers and bringing them into the house where I can focus on their beauty. They don't have to be perfect; indeed I love them more for their imperfections – their blotched leaves, their color-spotted petals and their earwigs. And without wishing to upset flower growers, the commercial roses sold by florists, with a few notable and expensive exceptions, bear no comparison with their magnificent garden relatives.

For a meager investment in one rose plant, you'll be picking fragrant garden roses for years to come. They may not be as perfectly straight and leggy in stem as commercially grown roses, but a couple of fulsome homegrown blooms popped into a jam jar will be infinitely more charming. Not only do garden roses unfurl fully in the vase – unlike so many florist's roses – they even fade and die with great style. Every bunch is a painterly still life.

The selection in this book serves as an inspirational introduction to the many forms of Vintage rose – the frilly tutu, the pleated masterpiece, the full-bodied and the modest five-petaled rose. The key information given here relates to how each rose performs in a temperate climate; in other conditions they are likely to behave differently – for example, they commonly grow somewhat taller in warmer climates. There are 39 National Rose Societies dotted around the world and they are a great source of information. Never underestimate the benefit of good local advice.

Some of the roses listed are old; some are very new. Some varieties are more readily obtainable than others. In all cases, I have listed an alternative variety with similar visual appeal. Don't be discouraged if you can't get ahold of the exact rose in your area – and remember that Internet shopping can make it much easier to find the precise variety you are looking for. Roses are cheapest bought bare root in winter, when they can be dispatched by mail.

I have deliberately steered clear of dividing the roses into technical classes such as Moss, Noisette or Hybrid Musk. I am more interested in the individual peculiarities of each rose and am not convinced that such a daunting level of information is entirely relevant if you are merely looking to plant a rose or two in your garden. Please use this as an inspirational source book; your knowledge and expertise will grow along with your roses.

One could argue that all roses are "vintage," since all have the genetic characteristics of their forebears and they do not grow true without human help. But not all take their style lead from the glorious Old rose. I could suggest that in developing the Hybrid Tea, we created something different, showier and inherently vulgar, but I am biased and such an assessment is not entirely fair. Hybrid Teas have their place and they excel on the show table, where their manicured sculptural perfection gains plaudits.

Hybrid Tea roses invaded and annexed suburban gardens in the late nineteenth and twentieth centuries, and nearly drove out their

gentler, beautiful old relatives. They dominated gardens, haunted my youth with their stiff form and bilious colors, and propagated the myth that rose growing is only for devoted fanatics. Without the supreme devotion of a few Old-rose fanciers and the inspirational work of a handful of innovative rose growers, the source of wondrous beauty that is the Old rose might have been lost.

This book is, therefore, a celebration of the Vintage rose – its seductive beauty, its ability to enhance our environment, its intoxicating perfume and its dramatic statements. Above all else, the book is designed to encourage you to plant your own roses, so that you, too, can share the sheer joy and delight of watching them bloom, of picking them and of bringing them into your home.

A SHORT HISTORY OF ROSES

THE ORIGIN OF ROSES IS SHROUDED IN MYSTERY. FOSSILIZED SPECIES OF ROSES HAVE BEEN FOUND ACROSS THE NORTHERN HEMISPHERE AND ARE ESTIMATED TO DATE BACK SOME 35–40 MILLION YEARS. THIS PLANT'S MANY FORMS HAVE SPRUNG FROM SOME 150 SPECIES OF WILD ROSE, THOUGH BOTANISTS DISPUTE THE PRECISE NUMBER. CHINA IS HOME TO HALF OF THESE AND BOASTS MORE ENDEMIC SPECIES THAN ANYWHERE ELSE IN THE WORLD, INDICATING THAT CHINA IS THE UNDOUBTED BIRTHPLACE OF THE ROSE. THE REMARKABLE BEAUTY, FRAGRANCE AND USEFULNESS OF THE ROSE HAVE GUARANTEED ITS SPREAD RIGHT ACROSS THE GLOBE. THROUGHOUT THE YEARS, ITS POTENT POWER HAS COME TO SYMBOLIZE MANY THINGS, BUT ABOVE ALL, THE ROSE IS A PLANT TO BE ENJOYED AND WONDERED AT.

To describe any rose as "vintage" is perhaps something of an understatement: roses were blooming long before humans walked the Earth. In China and North America, rose fossils have been found that date from the Eocene epoch, some 56 to 33.9 million years ago. Much more recently, roses were painted on Chinese pottery of 3500 BC and wild roses appear in *The Blue Bird* fresco on the walls of a Minoan townhouse in Knossos, which dates back to around 1550 BC.

Palace records from Pylos, in the Greek Peloponnese, date back to 1300 BC and reveal a trade in rose oil. The Greek historian Herodotus (c. 484–425 BC) recorded wild roses growing in ancient Thrace, in an area he called "the garden of Midas," and Theophrastus (c. 371–287 BC), a student of Aristotle and described by Linnaeus as the "father of botany," observed in his botanical text *Enquiry into Plants* the growing of both wild and cultivated roses, proving that roses were already happily mutating. Wilted rose garlands were found in Roman tombs in Hawara, Egypt, that date back to AD 170.

The Romans, in their turn, developed a passion for the rose. By the fall of Rome in AD 476, the empire boasted around 2000 rose gardens. The Romans used roses in myriad ways – warriors and statesmen garlanded their heads with wreaths of them and roses formed part of an array of potions and lotions designed to soothe the skin, ease toothaches and even, mixed with bear grease, as a remedy for baldness.

The Romans decorated the ceilings of their banqueting rooms with roses as a reminder that what was spoken while under the influence of wine was *sub rosa*, or "under the rose," and to be kept private and confidential. Thereafter, the rose was adopted by various religious and political groups, such as the Lutherans and the Rosicrucians, to symbolize faith and discretion.

Significantly, Roman writers began to advise on the cultivation of roses, with Marcus Terentius Vallo (116–27 BC) proposing that they be commercially cultivated, along with violets. In his *Natural History*, Pliny the Elder (AD 23–79) unhelpfully proposed that prior to planting roses, the ground should be dug deeper than for corn but not as deeply as for vines.

The origin of roses

All roses have their origins in the wild rose – such as the simple five-petaled Dog rose (*Rosa canina*) that seeds readily from hips and scrambles through hedgerows, ascending to great heights via thorny stems. This wild, or Species, rose grows true from seed when pollinated by its own species. Most such roses originated in Asia and North America.

Aside from these, some of the oldest cultivated roses are the multipetaled Gallicas. The Greeks and Romans grew *Rosa gallica* and it may well be this rose that features in one of the surviving murals in Pompeii.

According to legend, a cultivated form of *Rosa gallica* – *Rosa gallica* var. *officinalis* – traveled from Syria via Damascus to France, where it was dubbed the Rose of Provins, courtesy of Thibault of Navarre (1201–1253), who reputedly carried it back from the Crusades in his helmet. In all probability this rose was already in cultivation in Roman gardens. Despite the story of Thibault and the Crusades, *Rosa gallica* var. *officinalis* was certainly recorded in the court of Charlemagne in the ninth century, where it was used for perfumery and for medicinal purposes.

It was the medicinal and fragrant properties of *Rosa gallica* var. *officinalis* that accounted for the spread of that rose across Europe, probably via monastery gardens but also via the Moors and their gardens in the Iberian Peninsula. In England, the medicinal use of this same pinkish-red rose led to it being dubbed the Apothecary's rose.

And, according to research carried out by the English geneticist Charles Chamberlain Hurst (1870–1947), *Rosa gallica* var. *officinalis* is said to be the rose from which most of our garden varieties evolved. It is also cited as the rose of choice for potpourri.

Right A Shropshire Lad (see p. 138)

The rose as a symbol

Famously, this same *Rosa gallica* var. *officinalis* became the symbol of England's House of Lancaster (a branch of the House of Plantagenet) during the Wars of the Roses (1455–1487), though it was never officially registered as part of their insignia. The Lancaster claim to the throne came via Edward III, his son John of Gaunt, the Duke of Lancaster, and Katharine Sywnford, his mistress and later third wife. They were the great-grandparents of Margaret Beaufort, the mother of Henry Tudor, later Henry VII.

The Yorkists, another branch of the Plantagenets, adopted *Rosa alba*, a native white rose growing wild throughout Britain. The Yorkist claim to the throne came via Edward III, his son Edmund of Langley, Duke of York, and his wife Isabella of Castille. They were the great-grandparents of Edward IV of York and his brother King Richard III.

Henry Tudor defeated Richard III at the Battle of Bosworth (1485), took the throne of England and ended the Wars of the Roses by marrying Elizabeth of York, daughter of Edward IV and Elizabeth Woodville. This finally united the two warring Plantagenet factions and started the Tudor dynasty. To symbolize the unity and create a new, potent symbol, Henry VII amalgamated the red rose of Lancaster with the white rose of York to form the Tudor rose. (Interestingly, despite the Wars of the Roses, it was not until the nineteenth century that the counties of York and Lancaster started using red and white roses in any symbolic way.)

Henry VII's granddaughter, Elizabeth I, took the symbolism of the rose further, by adopting the sweet briar, or Eglantine (*Rosa eglanteria*, now known as *R. rubiginosa*), as her personal emblem. As can clearly be seen in portraits of Elizabeth by the miniaturist Nicholas Hilliard, she had her dresses smothered with embroidered sweet briar roses to remind onlookers of her dynastic power.

But the rose as a symbol had its origins long before its use as such in England in the fifteenth century. The early Christians regarded the rose as a pagan symbol and so frowned on it. It only emerged as a Christian symbol in the fourth century and would later appear in numerous incarnations, including a white thornless rose that represented the Virgin Mary and the red rose symbolizing the five wounds of Christ's Passion. These images were repeated countless times in the manuscripts, paintings, sculptures and carvings of the Middle Ages and the Renaissance.

At the same time, writers and poets used the rose to indicate both passion and women's sex and sexuality, most notably in the thirteenth-century "Roman de la Rose," an allegorical poem of chivalric love, cowritten by Guillame de Lorris and Jean de Meun.

Later on, of course, Shakespeare and Keats were also to use roses as a symbol of love, while, since World War Two, the red rose has become the symbol of social democracy and is used by political parties across Europe as well as in parts of Asia and the Americas.

Opposite Lovely Fairy (see p. 54)

The rose in modern times

The early development of cultivated roses is poorly recorded but can be deduced in part by looking at old books on gardening and at herbals (descriptions of medicinal plants).

There must have been a significant level of public interest in roses in England by the sixteenth century. In 1563, Thomas Hill published the first popular English book on gardening – *The proffitable Arte of Gardening: A most briefe and pleasaunte treatyse, teachynge how to dresse, sowe, and set a garden*, which details how to plant and care for roses.

John Gerard's *Herball, or Generall Historie of Plantes*, published in 1597, lists 14 roses. Just 30 years later the Royal Apothecary, John Parkinson, lists 24, while botanist, herbalist, physician and astrologer Nicholas Culpeper was less effusive, listing fewer rose varieties than this in his *Complete Herbal* of 1653.

The work of the Dutch and Flemish Old Masters provides visual evidence of the development of new roses in the Low Countries. In *Rariorum Plantarum Historia*, published in 1601, Flemish botanist Carolus Clusius records growing the hybrid *Rosa* x *centifolia* (later known as the Provence or Cabbage rose), sent to him as a piece of root by one Johan van Hoghelande. This rose was immortalized by Jacques de Gheyn II in a still life completed between 1600 and 1604. Later in the seventeenth century, during the Dutch Golden Age, painters such as Daniel Seghers and Jan Brueghel the Elder celebrated other new varieties.

It was in the seventeenth century that growers first recognized the lucrative possibilities of the rose. Since only wild roses grow true from seed, growers had become accustomed to propagate roses asexually by means of layering, taking cuttings or grafting. In this way they could create a perfect, identical copy of any rose.

Dutch growers soon realized that, through cross-pollination, they could encourage the rose to do what it does naturally and see what new varieties arose. Any new varieties could then be propagated by traditional methods. It proved a hit-and-miss system, for only one among many thousands of seedlings might have the distinctive qualities and individual characteristics that warranted the introduction and naming of a new variety. Despite this, between 1600 and 1720, Dutch growers introduced nearly 200 new varieties of rose, of which the luscious *Rosa* x *centifolia* may be the prime example.

In the seventeenth century, roses were not the desirable flowers they are today. Instead, tulips dominated people's attention; an enormous trade in tulips developed and fortunes were made – and lost – through speculation in tulip bulbs. Later, in the eighteenth century, post tulip-mania, pinks, primroses, peonies, chrysanthemums and camellias took over as the fashionable flowers of the day. Roses were probably regarded as a little old hat.

Fast forward to the early nineteenth century and the Empress Josephine of France. One of the great myths of this period is that Josephine created stunning rose gardens at her country house, the Château of Malmaison. However, the myth was blown apart by Jennifer Potter in her beautifully written and researched book, *The Rose* (2011). Potter points out that there is no evidence of a rose garden at Malmaison and that in the many breathless eulogies to the undoubtedly extravagant garden that did exist, there is no mention of any species of rose. This makes mockery of the oft-repeated claim that Josephine collected every known species of rose, though the garden undoubtedly did contain some roses.

Josephine's reputation as a rose connoisseur is in some small part due to one of the world's greatest painters of roses, Pierre-Joseph Redouté (1759–1840). A rose enthusiast, Redouté was Josephine's protégé and was appointed "Flower-Painter to the Empress." He trawled French rose gardens and the countryside looking for inspiration. The resulting work, *Les Roses*, a series of superb botanical illustrations that remain popular today, was published in three volumes between 1817 and 1824. It listed where the roses were found – but only two are attributed to Malmaison. What is more, Josephine died in 1814, three years before the publication of Redouté's work.

It was not until later in that century that nurseries and growers once again recognized the commercial potential of the rose. The initial experimental crossbreeding was between the familiar European *Rosa gallica*, *R. alba*, Damask roses (*Rosa x damascena*) and Centifolia roses. Later, these were crossbred with the exciting "new" (to Europe) China and Tea roses that had the advantage of being repeat-flowering.

The result was new classes of Noisette, Moss, Portland and Bourbon roses, from which sprang many thousands of hybrids in miniature, dwarf, shrub, climbing and rambling forms. Breeders were looking for novelty in form, color and fragrance, and through that, fame and financial gain. These new classes of rose became enormously popular – so much so that many of the old varieties fell from favor.

The impact of commerce

The eventual naming of roses was an effort on the part of breeders to establish their commercial rights to a rose. Through their choice of name, they could also compliment a sponsor, curry favor and even gain a little extra income, since growers started accepting payment for naming a rose after someone. (Formal patent legislation was introduced in America by the US Congress in 1930 with the Plant Patent Act; it was slower to arrive in the UK – the Plants Variety Rights Office was only set up in 1964.)

In 1867, Jean-Baptiste André Guillot Fils introduced La France, the first Hybrid Tea rose. This looks more like an Old rose than the vulgar, gaudy Hybrid Tea roses that my father cultivated so enthusiastically in the 1960s. (These so horrified my childish aesthetics that they nearly put me off roses for life.) The Hybrid Tea rose – recognized as a new class in 1879 – was so named because it was the result of an accidental cross between a Hybrid Perpetual and a Tea rose. It combined the beautiful form of the tender, repeat-flowering Tea rose with the strength and vigor of the Hybrid Perpetuals. Its introduction marks the birth of the modern rose.

The Hybrid Tea was hugely popular almost immediately. The flowers are large, beautifully formed, mostly fragrant, come in a huge range of colors – though a true blue rose still eludes breeders – and are borne on long stems.

Cross-pollination with Hybrid Teas then resulted in other new classes – the fabulous Floribundas, Shrub roses and Groundcover roses. Such was the success of these new classes that the sales of Old roses, as they were now dubbed, declined dramatically.

The subsequent revival of Old roses can be attributed to just a few committed English men and women. Garden designer Gertrude Jekyll (1843–1932) was influenced by the late nineteenth-century Arts and Crafts movement. She promoted a freer, painterly approach to planting, one more in tune with nature and the exact opposite of the style of planting favored by the Victorians, whose passion was for formal bedding schemes with serried ranks of Hybrid Teas.

Jekyll made a clear distinction between show roses that are grown for their blooms and garden roses – "the Old roses such as the Damask, Moss and Cabbage (or Provence) rose, and the Sweet Brier [*sic*] that blend harmoniously with other garden plants" – though she readily acknowledged that some show roses can have uses in the garden. Her colorist's eye favored the tender tones of what she described as the "modest" rose.

Vita Sackville-West (1892–1962) was another forceful advocate of Old roses. In 1930, this remarkable poet and novelist created her world-renowned garden at Sissinghurst in Kent. She adored Old roses, commenting once that "some of the Old roses demand an acquired taste before they can be appreciated as being a far quieter and more subtle thing than the highly colored Hybrid Teas, Polyanthas and Floribundas of the modern garden."

What began as a weekly hunt for the perfect boutonniere to wear to church had, by 1896, evolved into a startlingly outsize private collection of some 4000 roses for the Reverend Joseph Pemberton (1852–1926). In 1913, after a two-year stint as president of the National Rose Society, he set out to breed new varieties of roses that would keep on blooming until Christmas Day – unlike his grandmother's roses, which were finished by July. His legacy was, and still is, phenomenal,

Left Sally Holmes (see p. 80), Pink Gruss an Aachen
(see p. 41), Poulsen's Pearl and G. Nabonnand

for he created a new class of rose – the Hybrid Musks – vintage in style, but with the seductive capacity to bloom for months on end.

The English horticulturalist Graham Stuart Thomas (1909–2003) acknowledged that he was brought up on Hybrid Tea roses, which he loved but described as being "all about the flowers and not about the whole plant." While working at Hillings, a wholesale nursery in Surrey, he cycled to Munstead Wood, Gertrude Jekyll's home, and inveigled her into giving him an invitation to see the garden. In an unusually generous mood, she gave him a tour and so fostered his interest in the art of gardening.

Thomas said he was first introduced to Old roses on a visit to Ireland in 1937, after which they became his all-consuming passion. During World War Two he witnessed the sale of some rose collections and realized that many Old roses would soon be lost to commercial cultivation and thus, in time, lost forever.

Towards the end of the war he made the acquaintance of the florist Constance Spry, who had been assiduously collecting Old roses from French and American nurseries. Spry asked Thomas if he could propagate some of her roses to ensure their perpetuity. He became convinced that there was nothing to equal them and that they had been neglected by an entire generation. "A few prophets of the prewar days had been crying out in the wilderness," Thomas observed, "and a few keen spirits had preserved these beauties for our later enjoyment."

Thomas made it his life's work to preserve these Old roses and save them from extinction. He began working with the National Trust in 1948, when it acquired its first garden, Hidcote Manor, and in 1955 he wrote *The Old Shrub Roses* – the first of many books – in an effort to "bring forth these lovely things from retirement." He also promoted their commercial use, selling them in nurseries as quality products. His rose collection eventually found a home at Mottisfont Abbey when he laid out its now-acclaimed rose garden in 1974.

Combining the old with the new

The craving for novelty in roses has continued unabated for some 200 years but it is thanks to two great modern rosarians, Peter Beales and David Austin, that the focus was diverted to breeding new roses that celebrate the best features of the old ones.

Peter Beales, who worked under Graham Stuart Thomas at Hillings, opened his own nursery in 1968, collecting, breeding and writing about Old roses, as well as introducing cultivars of his own. His nursery also happens to hold the National Collection of wild Species roses.

David Austin, an inspired and influential rose breeder, is dedicated to developing new varieties with the charm and fragrance of Old roses, but Austin's roses repeat-flower and have good disease resistance. He has dubbed them "English Roses," though this name has not been officially recognized as a class by the rose authorities. Nevertheless, the term has come into common public use, and consumers know that "English roses" celebrate all that is best about Old roses.

Austin's first rose was the glorious Constance Spry, introduced in 1961. Today he runs one of the largest rose breeding programs in the world and sells worldwide. He has also specially bred a range of florists' roses that combine the beauty and fragrance of Old garden roses with the cut life of commercial florists' varieties. Traditional florists' roses are my personal *bête noire*; almost without exception they look as though they are destined for sale on a garage forecourt, so I thank David Austin for this exciting new development.

Graham Stuart Thomas confidently predicted that Hybrid Tea roses would fall from favor once roses were developed that combined the charm and beauty of Old roses with the vigor and fragrance of Hybrid Teas. It is fair to say that his prediction has come true, but the good news is, we still treasure and celebrate the old varieties too.

The uses of the rose

That the rose has nutritious properties is not a matter of dispute. It was a food source thousands of years ago – rose seeds were found among the remains of a Neolithic woman unearthed in Britain – and in the seventeenth century, botanist and herbalist John Gerard was promoting the use of rose hips as a culinary flavoring in junkets (milk-based desserts), cakes and sauces.

But it was not until the 1930s that rose hips were found to contain more vitamin C than any other fruit or vegetable – 20 times more than the same weight of oranges. During World War Two in Britain, when fruit and vegetable shortages began, a national campaign urged volunteers to collect hundreds of tons of rose hips. In an effort to keep the nation healthy, these were to be processed into rose-hip syrup to be diluted as a drink or to flavor desserts.

The essential oil from rose petals was believed to have medicinal properties, and it was used in massage oils – and later, aromatherapy – to aid circulation and cleanse the blood. This continues today. Similarly an infusion made from the petals continues to be used to make soothing anti-inflammatory compresses, notably for eye infections.

The fragrant properties of *Rosa damascena*, thought to hail from Persia and Egypt, were harnessed to produce attar of roses. It takes 250 lb (113 kg) of petals to produce 1 oz (28 g) of this essential oil, which is still used today in the production of luxury perfumes.

Left James Galway (see p. 166)

CLASSIC
BLOOMS

To some extent, all Vintage roses can be dubbed classics, since they are elegant, understated, timeless and enduring. Some, however, fit more neatly into this category. They exemplify their type in form – delicate single-flowered beauties, expansive cupped goblets, great overblown corsages, and frilled and pleated multipetaled fancies. Their hue is also significant. Neutral tones cannot automatically be classed as classic merely because they are pale, and not all intense colors shout noisily for our immediate attention. These roses all have a warmth in tone that subtly shifts through a harmonious palette from bud to maturity.

Old Blush China

The perfect cottage-garden rose,
Old Blush China, twiggy and light,
and with its relaxed blooms, blends
beautifully with other garden
flowers. Dubbed the "Monthly Rose,"
for its propensity to flower right
through from spring to autumn (year-
round in warmer climates), it's a valuable
garden plant, and in honor of these charms,
it entered the World Federation of Rose Societies
Old Rose Hall of Fame in 1988. Its buds are red,
opening to loose, pale pink double flowers
that blush to a warm pink as they mature.
The petals fold right back to reveal golden
yellow stamens. Old Blush China has
blooms in clusters of five and its flowers,
which have a sweet and pleasing fragrance,
reach a diameter of around 3 in (8 cm).

This rose can grow taller if the conditions suit – it likes warmth – and is
available in a climbing form with slightly larger flowers. It
needs blessedly little pruning; just deadhead and give a light trim to
keep it in shape – but stay your hand – and cut out old dead wood. Old
Blush China is also known as Parsons' Pink China in the UK, where it
was commercially introduced in 1793 by the astute Mr. Parsons. It has
been grown in China for over a thousand years and there goes by the name
of Yue Yue Fen – which translates as "Monthly Pink." It is something of a
matriarch – the genes of Old Blush China are found in most modern roses.

Old Blush China

Flowering Repeat-flowers from spring into autumn
Aspect Sunny but will tolerate partial shade
Soil Rich, moist and well drained
Habit Tall bush
Average height 39–200 in (1–5 m)
Average spread 39 in (1 m)
Pruning Restraint is the order
Foliage Red when young, turning midgreen
Thorns Some
As a cut flower Relaxed and charming
Similar varieties Sophie's Perpetual; Hermosa

Buff Beauty

Buff Beauty is acclaimed as one of the most popular of the Hybrid Musks and is a deserved award-winner. Not only does it have a wonderful Tea-rose fragrance but it produces great trusses of blooms in generous clusters. The color of the flowers is perfection itself; the buds are a pale buttery yellow, opening to apricot-yellow, multipetaled double and semidouble flowers that fade to a creamy buff. It flowers in summer and again in early autumn; the later flowers are stronger in hue but blooms vary in shade according to temperature and position.

Buff Beauty mixes superbly with other plants, discreetly offsetting many other shades of rose as well as mixed plantings. Grown against a wall, it can reach generous proportions in warm climates. It also has the advantage of being relatively disease free. Ann Bentall introduced the rose in 1939, though it is thought that it might have been bred by the revered Reverend Joseph Hardwick Pemberton (see p. 21), the famous vicar-turned-rose-grower.

Flowering Repeat-flowers
Aspect Sunny but will tolerate partial shade
Soil Moist and well drained
Habit Arching shrub or climber in warm climates
Average height 59 in (1.5 m)
Average spread 59 in (1.5 m)
Pruning Flourish your secateurs (pruning clippers). Give it a main pruning in late autumn and prune again lightly in midsummer to encourage a second flowering in early autumn
Foliage Copper when young, turning dark green; semievergreen in some climates
Thorns Some
As a cut flower Exquisite and classy
Similar varieties Gloire de Dijon

Celsiana

You can't beat a good old-fashioned pink rose and Celsiana has a long and excellent pedigree. It was painted by Redouté, which in my book is always the mark of a beautiful flower. It buds sugar pink and the feathery, artful sepals open to generous clusters of 7–15 sweet, pink, semidouble flowers that fade prettily with age, nodding and bowing on long stems. The informal ruffled, papery blooms can reach a diameter of around 3½ in (9 cm) and have a strong, delicious perfume that hangs in the air. The petals fold right back to reveal a halo of golden stamens that are delicately tipped with brown in maturity. Some small hips may be produced in autumn.

Tough as old boots and able to withstand some seriously harsh winters – up to an impressive −22°F (−30°C) – Celsiana should be deadheaded to promote repeat-flowering. You should also trim out some old wood annually but don't go crazy as it flowers on the old wood. A light prune is what is required.

Celsiana's true origin is unknown but it was named by the French botanist Claude-Antoine Thory, who worked on the genealogy of roses, reputedly in honor of his compatriot, the distinguished plantsman Jacques Philippe Martin Cels.

Flowering Repeats and repeats
Aspect Sunny but will tolerate partial shade
Soil Rich, moist and well drained
Habit Tall shrub
Average height 79 in (2 m)
Average spread 59 in (1.5 m)
Pruning Light
Foliage Gray green
Thorns Small thorns
As a cut flower Excellent and informal
Similar varieties Georgetown Noisette

Irène Watts
Pink Gruss an Aachen

Here's a small but perfectly formed rose that is clouded in confusion and mystery. Mottisfont Abbey, home to one of the world's most beautiful rose gardens, accidentally mislabeled Pink Gruss an Aachen as Irène Watts – we are all fallible. As a result, many roses that are sold in the USA as Irène Watts are actually Pink Gruss an Aachen. A curator at Mottisfont owned up to the error in the 1990s but by that time the actual Irène Watts had become elusive. The original breeder of Irène Watts, one Pierre Guillot, introduced it in 1896 but even his family's nursery, though still flourishing, no longer stocks this rose. Even its name is a mystery; we do not know definitively who Irène Watts was, nor why she had a rose named after her.

But let's not be picky. Both Irène Watts and its virtual doppelganger Pink Gruss an Aachen are exceptionally lovely roses. The deep pink buds appear in clusters of 3–11 and open to glorious double flowers with a mass of sweet peachy-pink petals that pale to the outer edges. The color is variable, depending on climate and season. The flowers, which reach a diameter of 2¾ in (7 cm), have a sweet perfume. This rose performs well in containers and is a delight at the front of a mixed border.

Flowering Repeat-flowers
Aspect Sunny but will tolerate partial shade
Soil Rich, moist and well drained
Habit Diminutive shrub
Average height 32 in (80 cm)
Average spread 23½ in (60 cm)
Pruning Light
Foliage Dark to midgreen
Thorns Few
As a cut flower Fills a room with perfume
Similar varieties Gruss an Aachen

Penelope

Penelope is a deliciously blowsy, full-blown rose, reminiscent of the kind that was used to decorate hats, or more latterly, the fabric corsages popularized by Sarah Jessica Parker in the television series *Sex and the City*.

The flower buds are a coppery pink, fading to pale shell pink as the ruffled petals start to unfurl, and paling to white as they fold right back to reveal a yellow heart, bursting with splendid lemon-yellow stamens. This is a proper garden rose – not one you'd find in a florist's shop – and all the lovelier for it.

One of the most reliable of the Hybrid Musks, Penelope is imbued with a lovely musky sweet fragrance, as you'd expect. A bush rose that will grow to around 59–79 in (1.5–2 m), it can be even taller in warm climates, where it can turn into a climber. The bushes are smothered with flowers in large clusters and it repeat-flowers, doing particularly well in the early autumn if you deadhead it through the summer. If you leave the flowers to fade at the end of the summer, you'll be rewarded with some startlingly bright, coral-pink hips.

Penelope is tolerant of shade and can withstand poor soil if it must. It was created in 1924 by the Reverend Joseph Hardwick Pemberton (see p. 21), who wanted to re-create the roses he remembered as a child.

Flowering Repeat-flowers
Aspect Tolerant; can cope with all aspects
Soil Tolerant; ideally well drained and moist
Habit Bushy shrub or climber in warm climates
Average height 59 in (1.5 m)
Average spread 39 in (1 m)
Pruning Not required
Foliage Dark red when young, turning dark green and glossy
As a cut flower Enjoy the subtly fading hues that a whole bunch provides
Similar varieties Sally Holmes

Lady Hillingdon

Lady Hillingdon (1857–1940) is perhaps best remembered for purportedly coining the phrase "lie back and think of England." She reputedly used it in 1912, either in her journal or in a somewhat revealing letter to her mother, in reference to enduring her husband's twice-weekly visits to her "bedchamber." The Lady Hillingdon rose was introduced in 1910, two years before Lady H. made her pithy observation, by the rose breeders Lowe and Shawyer. Their nursery was in Uxbridge and ironically they named the rose after Lady Hillingdon as a mark of respect to her husband – the second Baron of Hillingdon and a Conservative politician, whose family home (Hillingdon Court) was in Uxbridge. Elisha J. Hicks, an English breeder, introduced the climbing form – a sport of its parent – in 1917.

Perhaps best known as a climber, Lady Hillingdon buds a warm coppery yellow and throws out an endless succession of cupped buttery yellow flowers that fade with age. The cupped flowers reach a diameter of around 4 in (10 cm) and curl back revealing a halo of copper-yellow stamens. The blooms, which come in clusters of 3–7, have a strong Tea-rose scent and nod and bend their heavy heads on slender stems – perfect for climbing roses as they can be admired from below.

Lady Hillingdon blooms on new wood, so initially train the whips, tying them in where you want them to grow and fanning them out so they don't grow vertically, which encourages flowering. After the second or third year, prune out any dead or damaged wood in winter and tie in strong new shoots in the same way.

Flowering Repeat-flowers
Aspect Sunny
Soil Rich, moist and well drained
Habit Bush or climber
Average height 39 in (1 m) shrub; 158 in (4 m) climber
Average spread 23½ in (60 cm)
Pruning Remove dead and diseased wood
Foliage Copper when young; dark green in maturity
Thorns Yes
As a cut flower Long lasting and perfumed
Similar varieties Gloire de Dijon

Comte de Chambord

This is a sugar-pink marvel of a rose, a giant corsage of sweet fragrant delight. It buds a dusty rose pink and unfurls to a glorious, cupped, papery tutu of double-petaled blooms that can reach an impressive 4 in (10 cm) in diameter. With a color that's a world away from a harsh pink, it pales and fades to its outer petals, and does so still more with maturity. With its loose quartering, it's not a perfect bloom but is all the more charming for its relaxed style. The buds can ball but since it flowers so regularly, simply snip off any recalcitrant ones and wait for the next flush of blooms.

Comte de Chambord was introduced in 1863 by Robert et Moreau but, despite its honorable vintage, didn't gain a Royal Horticultural Society Award of Garden Merit until 1993. It was named after the splendidly titled Henri Charles Ferdinand Marie Dieudonné d'Artois, duc de Bordeaux and comte de Chambord (1820–83), the last legitimate male heir of Louis XV of France.

Flowering Repeat-flowers
Aspect Sunny
Soil Rich, moist and well drained
Habit Upright shrub
Average height 69 in (1.75 m)
Average spread 49 in (1.25 m)
Pruning Flowers on new wood so prune early
Foliage Midgreen
Thorns Yes, plenty
As a cut flower Hard to beat
Similar varieties Ispahan

Rosa rugosa Hansa

A splendidly sturdy Rugosa with good resistance to disease and with great, overblown, reddish-purple flowers that reach around 4 in (10 cm) in diameter. These flowers unfurl from a long curl of a bud and open into a relaxed chaos of petals. This is no perfect nursery flower but an utterly charming bloom with an intense and delicious fragrance – a perfect cottage-garden flower. The blooms are followed by a glorious flush of round, red hips.

Prune to keep growth in check if required; this rose is a good choice for hedging. Schaum and Van Tol of the Hansa Nursery introduced it in the Netherlands in 1905.

Flowering Repeat-flowers
Aspect Sunny
Soil Tolerant but ideally prefers rich, moist, well-drained soil
Habit Large shrub
Average height 79 in (2 m)
Average spread 59 in (1.5 m)
Pruning Cut out old stems
Foliage Light green
Thorns Be ready with gloves and goggles
As a cut flower A charming old-fashioned rose
Similar varieties Roseraie de l'Hay

Baronne Prévost

Bred by the amateur rose grower M. Desprez of Yèbles in France, and introduced in 1842, Baronne Prévost was one of the first Hybrid Perpetuals – a hybrid that repeat-flowers. And what flowers and what perfume! The fat pink buds open to luxuriant blooms that can unfurl to a heady 4 in (10 cm) diameter, multipetaled extravagance set against the bright green foliage. The flowers are a rich sugary pink in tone, fading with maturity to rose or lilac pink. The petals are quartered and in the heart you'll catch a glimpse of a tiny yellow button eye.

This rose benefits from a light prune in late summer to encourage repeat-flowering. It suits a relaxed setting, which makes it an ideal rose for a cottage garden. However, Baronne Prévost's performance varies depending on climate: it grows more luxuriantly in warm environments but is somewhat susceptible to black spot in cooler climates. Remove dead and diseased wood in winter and give it a light prune to improve the interior architecture for a rounded, open look.

It is a greedy plant but if you feed it, you will reap the reward in blooms. Baronne Prévost was awarded the Royal Horticultural Society's Award of Garden Merit in 1993.

Flowering Repeat-flowers
Aspect Thrives in warm climates but will tolerate partial shade
Soil Rich; manure regularly
Habit Sturdy, compact, upright growth; taller in warm climates
Average height 59 in (1.5 m)
Average spread 39 in (1 m)
Pruning Light summer pruning ensures repeat-flowering and controls growth
Foliage Bright green, forming a ruff beneath the flowers
Thorns Red thorns on rather prickly stems
As a cut flower A stunner – and fragrant with it
Similar varieties Jacques Cartier

Lovely Fairy

It doesn't get going early, but when it does, this diminutive pink rose is simply smothered in clusters of sugar-pink flowers from summer into autumn. It buds a warm pink, opening to double flowers that reach just 1 in (2.5 cm) in diameter, and which appear in candy floss clusters of 10–40 blooms. It's pretty in cottage gardens and is a good ground-cover plant.

Dying blooms tend to cling on to the plant, so you need to indulge in some deadheading every so often if you want to keep Lovely Fairy looking her best; this will also encourage repeat-flowering. If you're impatient, a very light trim with a pair of shears will do the trick. Every winter, cut back a proportion of the older stems quite hard to encourage the production of new shoots, which will flower the next summer. But all in all, this rose is an absolute breeze to grow.

The parent of this Polyantha rose, The Fairy, was introduced in 1932, but it was another 58 years before its sport, Lovely Fairy, was introduced by the Dutch breeder Vurens-Spek.

Flowering Repeat-flowers
Aspect Sunny
Soil Rich, moist and well drained
Habit Low and spreading
Average size 20 in (50 cm)
Average spread 39 in (1 m)
Pruning Cut around one-third of the old wood down close to the base and reduce the length of new growth by one-third
Foliage Green and glossy
Thorns Some
As a cut flower Short stemmed but pretty
Similar varieties The Fairy

Perle d'Or

This is a dainty, diminutive, deliciously hued flower that throws out masses of flowers and repeats in flushes. The warm, flesh-pink buds are perfectly formed and open into similarly perfectly formed creamy pink flowers. These unfurl further to a flat chaos of petals, with the outer petals paling to cream and with a fleshy, curling pink heart. The flowers are borne in great clustered bouquets of 5–15 flowers, reaching a diameter of just 1½ in (4 cm) and exuding a strong, sweet fragrance.

This is an amiable, tolerant, rewarding shrub, which can withstand some shade. Grown in poor soil, the flowers will have fewer petals and will open to reveal the stamens. Feed it and it will repay you handsomely. Deadhead, and prune lightly to shape.

Perle d'Or took the Royal Horticultural Society's Award of Garden Merit in 1993. There appears to be some debate as to whether it was raised by Joseph Rambaux or his splendidly named widow, Veuve Rambaux. Either way, it was introduced by their son-in-law, Francis Dubreuil, in 1883. For some inexplicable reason it is also known as the Yellow Cécile Brünner; while it does resemble this flower in form, it could never be described as yellow. The literal translation of its name – pearl of gold – indicates a much subtler colorist's interpretation.

Flowering Repeat-flowers
Aspect Sunny but will tolerate shade
Soil Rich, moist and well drained
Habit Arching shrub
Average height 39 in (1 m)
Average spread 39 in (1 m)
Pruning Light
Foliage Rich dark green
Thorns A few disproportionately outsized thorns
As a cut flower Deliciously scented
Similar varieties Cécile Brünner

Constance Spry

It may only flower once – but oh, what a rose! Fragrant and outsized, this is a dazzlingly beautiful bloom. Graham Stuart Thomas (see p. 23), the famous English horticulturalist and rose connoisseur, described its fragrance as being like myrrh, but he was not a perfumer. Myrrh has a familiar but curiously earthy smell; in Constance Spry, the notes of myrrh are subtly mixed with those of Old rose to produce an exquisite, spicy, heady perfume that hangs in the air.

It buds dark pink, opening into a great globe of a flower of the sweetest pink that reaches an impressive diameter of around 5¼ in (13 cm). Paling as it unfurls, Constance Spry reveals a globular bloom with exquisite incurving petals reminiscent of a peony. At the heart is a halo of golden stamens that are rarely fully revealed. The flowers are borne singly or in clusters of up to six blooms; they nod their heads on slender stems, wafting their glorious perfume.

This tall shrub, which also comes as a climber, may bloom only once in midsummer but it is positively smothered in flowers. Pick and deadhead with a vengeance and prune lightly in winter. Feed it freely to encourage the great flush of blooms.

As a cut flower, Constance Spry is exquisite, though it starts shedding its petals within a couple of days of being picked. It blooms profusely for around three weeks and is so very lovely that you will lose your heart to it.

Constance Spry was David Austin's (see p. 25) very first rose – the archetypical "English Rose." He named it in tribute to the great florist Constance Spry OBE, who championed natural flower arranging and who had a particular fondness for Old roses. Spry arranged the flowers for Princess Elizabeth's wedding to Prince Philip in 1947, and also for her coronation as Queen Elizabeth II in 1953. This rose was introduced in 1961 by Roses and Shrubs of Albrighton and Sunningdale Nurseries, before David Austin Roses Ltd. was formed in 1969.

Flowering Once in midsummer
Aspect Sunny
Soil Rich, moist and well drained
Habit Vigorous, arching shrub
Average height 98 in (2.5 m)
Average spread 59 in (1.5 m)
Pruning Light in autumn
Foliage Midgreen and large
Thorns Lots of small thorns
As a cut flower Hard to better
Similar varieties Princess Alexandra of Kent; Gertrude Jekyll

Desdemona

Desdemona is a superb example of a classic rose – the color works with everything in the garden, and as a cut flower it is the picture of elegance, equally effective alone or as a neutral foil in all kinds of flower arrangements. Launched in 2015 by the indefatigable David Austin (see p. 25), Desdemona buds a pale pink with a darker tip. It opens into a charming chalice of petals, imbued with the palest hint of creamy pink and paling as the incurving petals unfurl to a creamy white, then fade again to white. It creates a wondrous ensemble of shades of white that are influenced by the light and surrounding colors. At the heart you can catch a glimpse of the sulfur stamens. The flowers, which reach 3½ in (9 cm) in diameter, have a strong fragrance with hints of myrrh. They bloom from early summer until the first frosts. Desdemona's flowers are apparently indifferent to rain, which is a huge bonus in a wet climate.

Austin named this rose after William Shakespeare's pure and innocent heroine from his tragedy *Othello*.

Flowering Repeat-flowers
Aspect Sunny
Soil Rich, moist and well drained
Habit Open, upright shrub
Average height 48 in (1.2 m)
Average spread 35 in (90 cm)
Pruning Light pruning initially; remove about one-third thereafter
Foliage Dark green and glossy
Thorns Yes
As a cut flower Utterly charming and fragrant
Similar varieties Lichfield Angel; Tranquillity (see p. 152)

Eglantyne

This dusty pink bud opens to a sumptuous pale pink confusion of folded, pleated and cupped petals. It appears in clusters of 3–9 blooms that fade prettily with age. The flowers, which reach a diameter of 4 in (10 cm), have a delicious Old-rose fragrance. At their heart is a small green button eye, half concealed by a frill of tiny petals.

Prune this rose in winter and cut back the flowering stems by one-quarter after flowering. Feed generously.

David Austin (see p. 25) introduced Eglantyne in 1994, naming it in tribute to Eglantyne Jebb, who launched the esteemed charity Save the Children in May 1919, in the aftermath of World War One. Don't confuse this rose with *Rosa rubiginosa*, otherwise known as *R. eglanteria*, eglantine or sweet briar; that one is a wild rose with single pink blooms that becomes a bit of a giant.

Flowering Repeat-flowers
Aspect Sunny
Soil Rich, moist and well drained
Habit Upright shrub
Average height 49 in (1.25 m)
Average spread 39 in (1 m)
Pruning In winter
Foliage Midgreen
Thorns Yes; large and small
As a cut flower A perfect wedding flower
Similar varieties Mary Rose

Eglantyne with Gentle Hermione, Lady Emma Hamilton (see p. 212) and Graham Thomas (see p. 72)

Graham Thomas

Graham Stuart Thomas (see p. 23) was a man who knew his roses, and when he chose this one to bear his name, from a selection proffered by his friend David Austin (see p. 25), he knew what he was doing. Irrepressibly cheerful in hue, it is a superb golden yellow rose with hints of apricot, paling as it ages but never with any harsh or sharp lemon tones. Obliging in disposition, it throws out blooms from late spring until the first frosts but will determinedly continue to try to produce the odd bloom as late as Christmas Day if conditions are favorable.

The buds appear streaked and flushed with red, unfurling to cupped double flowers. These grow in clusters of 3–9 blooms and reach a diameter of 4½ in (11 cm). The flowers have a strong tea fragrance with fruity and floral notes.

The shrub grows tall so you have to be quite ruthless if you want to contain it. In warmer climates it makes an attractive climber.

Graham Thomas was voted the World's Favorite Rose in 2009 by members of the 39 National Rose Societies worldwide, and it was also awarded the Royal Horticultural Society's Award of Garden Merit in 1993. It was named as a tribute to British horticulturalist and influential gardener Graham Stuart Thomas, a champion of Old roses and a leading light in their revival. Thomas designed the world-famous rose garden at Mottisfont Abbey in Hampshire, using much of his personal collection.

Graham Thomas in a bouquet with *Clematis* 'The President', Walker's Low catmint (*Nepeta* x *faassenii* 'Walker's Low'), columbine, hardy geranium, hellebore and allium

Flowering Repeats and repeats
Aspect Sunny
Soil Rich, moist and well drained
Habit Bushy, upright shrub
Average height 59 in (1.5 m)
Average spread 48 in (1.2 m)
Pruning Keep it in check
Foliage Midgreen
Thorns Yes
As a cut flower Joyous
Similar varieties The Poet's Wife

Pierre de Ronsard

This is a glorious spun-sugar confection of a rose, a multilayered swirl of petals in a froth of delicious cream, white and powder-pink tones, with a hint of green on the outer petals. The color is variable but is always a blend of these charming tones. It buds a pale, pale green tipped with raspberry. The petals unfurl slowly over a period of days to reveal great cupped double blooms brimming over with curls of petals. The heavy flowers, which nod on their stems, reach an impressive 4 in (10 cm) in diameter and have a light fragrance.

This rose demands two things: sunshine – it really does best in a Mediterranean climate – and patience. It is slow growing but worth the wait as it is simply smothered in flowers in its first flush of blooms. In cool, wet climates, the blooms often fail to open fully.

Pierre de Ronsard was introduced by Marie-Louise Meilland in France in 1987. It is also known as Eden Rose, Eden 88 and Eden Climber. It was dubbed the World's Favorite Rose in 2006. Meilland named it in honor of the sixteenth-century French poet Pierre de Ronsard, who wrote the poem "The Rose" in 1551.

Flowering Repeat-flowers
Aspect Sunny
Soil Rich, moist and well drained
Habit Climber or shrub, depending on climate
Average height 119 in (3 m)
Average spread 79 in (2 m)
Pruning Tie in the young canes to the shape you want
Foliage Red when young, turning dark green and glossy
Thorns Few
As a cut flower Stunning – wait for the compliments
Similar varieties James Galway

Pierre de Ronsard (center), Leonardo da Vinci
(see p. 127), Mon Jardin et Ma Maison (see p. 162)
and Polka

Pierre de Ronsard, Leonardo da Vinci (see p. 127),
Mon Jardin et Ma Maison (see p. 162) and Polka

Sally Holmes

Sally Holmes, named after the grower's wife, was introduced in 1976. The buds are pale pink and unfurl into simple, refined flowers with wavy-edged petals and golden yellow stamens at their heart. The flowers, which reach a diameter of around 3 in (8 cm) and exude a light musky fragrance, simply smother the plant, and do so especially heavily at the top of the stems.

In cool climates, Sally Holmes is a large shrub, but in warm climates it can become a climber that flowers incessantly. Black spot can be a problem.

Flowering Repeat-flowers
Aspect Sunny
Soil Rich, moist and well drained
Habit Bushy shrub or climber
Average height 59 in (1.5 m)
Average spread 79 in (2 m)
Pruning Blooms on new wood; cut back by around one-third and tie in new growth horizontally
Foliage Midgreen
Thorns Few
As a cut flower Best enjoyed in the garden
Similar varieties Kew Gardens; Penelope

Iceberg

A classic white rose, hugely popular for its clusters of pretty flowers that repeat-bloom throughout the season. It entered the Rose Hall of Fame in 1983 after being voted the World's Favorite Rose by the World Federation of Rose Societies. It buds a pale shell pink, unfurling into a delicately shaped rose with a hint of pale pink, then opening further still to display fully white petals with a halo of golden stamens at their heart. The flowers, which have a light fruity fragrance, come in clusters of 3–15 blooms and reach a diameter of around 3 in (8 cm). As the summer advances, the petals acquire a pink hue or become freckled with the palest splashes of pink.

This is a tall shrub, which will reach climbing proportions in a warm climate. It also comes in a climbing form. It is subject to black spot.

Iceberg, also known as Schneewittchen and Fée des Neiges, was introduced in 1958 by the German rose grower Reimer Kordes.

Flowering Repeat-flowers
Aspect Sunny
Soil Rich, moist and well drained
Habit Tall shrub or climber
Average height 39 in (1 m)
Average spread 39 in (1 m)
Pruning Cut back to your required height
Foliage Dark green and semievergreen
Thorns Some
As a cut flower Pretty but short lived
Similar varieties Lichfield Angel

DRAMATIC
FLOWERS

Vintage roses may not be overtly dramatic by nature but some have a distinctive and commanding presence. Intensity of color draws the eye – the rich reds, the dark purples, the blowsy pinks, the golds, the deep copper-infused oranges and the hints of blue. Eye-catching forms, such as giant overblown blooms or drop-dead gorgeous, heavily petaled confections, simply beg for attention, as do roses that put forth a multitude of blooms in one stupendous show. Others have outstanding features, such as the irrepressible Rosa Mundi (see p. 88) and the intense Variegata di Bologna (see p. 100), both of which are prettily striped and freckled. Then there are roses such as Ellen Willmott (see p. 94), whose sensational golden anthers topped with red filaments cry out for close scrutiny. These striking roses are poseurs with attitude – the true supermodels of the garden.

Tuscany Superb

This Gallica is a rose I cannot live without. The flower buds are a dark maroon, with pretty layered sepals that unfurl to reveal a chaotic rosette of a catholic-purple intensity that darkens as it ages, and which can reach 3 in (8 cm) in diameter. The overall effect is of deep, dark, purple-red flowers that are a glorious muddle of unruly curls, with smaller multipetals clustering untidily in the heart. If the flowers unfurl efficiently, which they often don't, there is a stunning cloud of golden stamens at their center. The inner petals sometimes have a white flash, which offsets the stamens. It has a light but pleasing perfume.

Tuscany Superb was given the Royal Horticultural Society's Award of Garden Merit in 1993.

Reputedly bred prior to 1837 by the English fruit grower Thomas Rivers, this rose really appreciates a good mulch of well-rotted manure every winter. It can sulk and produce few flowers if left hungry. Mine rampaged through a beautiful olive tree, offsetting the silvery foliage with dark purple accents. Although it flowers but once, in my experience it will continue to throw out the odd bloom for some time. These are so exquisite that I snatch them from the plant and bring them into the house to take pole position on the kitchen table.

Flowering Once in summer
Aspect Sunny
Soil Rich, moist and well drained
Habit Vigorous, untidy shrub
Average height 59 in (1.5 m)
Average spread 49 in (1.25 m)
Pruning Prune gently to shape; it blooms on old wood
Foliage Dark green
Thorns Few
As a cut flower A stylish, long-lived rose that sheds its petals prettily
Similar varieties Tuscany; Munstead Wood (see p. 220); Cardinal de Richelieu

Rosa Mundi

Properly known as *Rosa gallica versicolor*, this rose has a genetic mutation that disrupts normal pigment development; as a result, no two petals or flowers are exactly alike. Rosa Mundi produces pale pink petals splashed, striped and freckled with spots of a dark pink. The buds are red and unfurl to semidouble ruffled flowers with a pretty burst of golden stamens at their heart. You may find the occasional flower is a plain sugar pink; this happens when it reverts to the hue of its parent. The blooms are deeply fragrant and can reach up to 4 in (10 cm) in diameter. Flowers are followed by oval red hips in late summer.

Rosa Mundi is a sport of *Rosa gallica* var. *officinalis*, the Apothecary's rose (see p. 14). Its true origin is unknown but it was first recorded in 1583 and was dubbed Rosa mundi in England, which means "rose of the world." In France it is known as Provins Panaché.

Rosa Mundi is a bushy shrub that can be grown as hedging. If you give it a mulch of well-rotted manure in winter, it will thank you with flowers. It is a robust plant, but like many Old roses can be susceptible to black spot and mildew. It was given the Royal Horticultural Society's Award of Garden Merit in 1993.

Flowering Once in high summer
Aspect Sunny but will tolerate partial shade
Soil Rich, moist and well drained but will tolerate poor soil
Habit Vigorous, bushy shrub
Average height 48 in (1.2 m)
Average spread 48 in (1.2 m)
Pruning Can be pruned hard with a hedge trimmer after flowering
Foliage Midgreen and rough
Thorns A few prickly bristles
As a cut flower Sweetly eye catching
Similar varieties Variegata di Bologna

Belvedere

This is a rose that goes by many names. In the United Kingdom it was dubbed Belvedere by the horticulturalist Graham Stuart Thomas (see p. 23) after it was discovered by Lady Rosse in the gardens of Belvedere House in County Westmeath, in Ireland.

Thomas maintains it was a spontaneous seedling but others believe it is actually Princesse Marie, a Sempervirens hybrid originating in France in 1929 and created by Antoine Jacques, who named it after his employer, the second daughter of King Louis-Phillipe.

Either way, it is a truly spectacular monster of a rose. It scrambles high, up and over walls and arches, and through trees. When it blooms, clouds of small pale pink cupped flowers that fade with age are preceded by great clusters of pale pink buds. The whole combines to create a staggering display of visual perfection. The only downside is that the blooms spoil in the rain, so it benefits from locations where summers are drier. Despite this failing, it is such a stunning plant that it took the Royal Horticultural Society's Award of Garden Merit in 2012.

Flowering Once
Aspect Sunny
Soil Rich, moist and well drained; feed annually
Habit Rampant rambler
Average height 236 in (6 m) and more in favorable conditions
Average spread 119 in (3 m)
Pruning Prune back in winter when it gets too big
Foliage Dark green
Thorns Yes
As a cut flower Very pretty floating en masse in water
Similar varieties Adélaïde d'Orléans

Ellen Willmott

There are many reasons for selecting a rose as distinctive, but it's not often the stamens that are its distinguishing feature. In some ways this is a gloriously simplistic and fragrant rose; the peachy buds open to reveal five scalloped pale pink petals that form a bloom with a diameter of 3 in (8 cm) and fade to creamy white. In cooler weather, the very tips of the petals are washed with a pale pink hue. But at the heart of the flower is its true glory – lengthy crimson filaments tipped with golden yellow anthers. Author and rose-grower Daphne Filiberti observed, "If roses had eyelashes, this one could certainly bat her eyes."

This is an upright Hybrid Tea rose, so you need to pick your planting spot carefully and surround it with herbaceous plants that will loosen up the overall effect.

Dubbed "the greatest of all living gardeners" by Gertrude Jekyll (see p. 21), Ellen Willmott, author of the book *The Genus Rosa*, was passionate about wild-rose species. This rose was introduced by William Archer in 1936, two years after Ellen Willmott's death. Archer, a furniture designer and amateur rose grower, was not alone in choosing to honor Willmott; over 60 plant cultivars and species were named after her.

Flowering Repeat-flowers
Aspect Sunny
Soil Rich, moist and well drained
Habit Upright
Average height 59 in (1.5 m)
Average spread 39 in (1 m)
Pruning Reduce by one-half to one-third annually
Foliage Red when young, turning dark green
Thorns Yes
As a cut flower Looks good on its long stems
Similar varieties Dainty Bess

Ellen Willmott with Blue for You (see p. 124), Magenta (see p. 129) and Fighting Temeraire (see p. 104)

François Debreuil

If you're looking for dark, velvet-red blooms, then François Debreuil is the rose for you. The long, conical buds are a deep, dark red and open into wonderful full-blown roses of intense shadowy red without a hint of tonal vulgarity. This rose has no artificial perfection in its blooms but is a great chaotic beauty, with nodding heads of fat, multipetaled flowers that pale a little with age to a defiant deep red. The occasional petal bears a tiny brushstroke of white. You are unlikely to catch more than a hint of the golden stamens at its heart.

François Debreuil is an exceptionally fragrant rose and will bloom in flushes throughout the summer. The rather twiggy growth struggles to support the fat flowers. This Tea rose was bred by its namesake, a tailor from Lyons who took up rose breeding. It was introduced in 1894.

Flowering Repeat-flowers from late spring
Aspect Sunny; will not tolerate shade
Soil Rich, moist and well drained
Habit Spreading, twiggy shrub or small climber
Average height 35 in (90 cm)
Average spread 23½ in (60 cm)
Pruning Prune to simplify the interior architecture in autumn or winter
Foliage Dark green and glossy but rather thin
Thorns Yes
As a cut flower Superb flowers borne on long stems
Similar varieties Munstead Wood

Variegata di Bologna

Variegata di Bologna is a petaled flurry of couture fancifulness. The dark pink buds open to reveal an exuberance of white petals, all flecked and striped with raspberry-pink detailing. The inner petals are washed with a pale, pale pink. Every single petal and every flower is different from each other. The flowers are fulsome, double and cupped, and have to be seen to be believed – no description ever quite does them justice. Like a tennis player's frilly knickers, they have an air of innocent sauciness. The flowers have a strong sweet perfume and open to a diameter of 3 in (8 cm). Variegata di Bologna is grown for the exceptional quality of each flower. Get picking!

Variegate di Bologna is a sport of its parent, Victor Emmanuel; occasionally it can revert and produce plain purple roses. This Bourbon rose was introduced in 1909 by Massimilano Lodi of Gaetano Bonfiglioli e figlio, from Bologna in Italy. Variegata di Bologna can take a few years to get going; be patient with it and feed it in winter. It can be susceptible to black spot.

Flowering Once strongly, then with a small repeat of blooms
Aspect Sunny; will not tolerate shade
Soil Rich, moist and well drained
Habit Shrub or can be trained to climb
Average height 71 in (1.8 m)
Average spread 59 in (1.5 m)
Pruning Leave for a few years to allow the flowering stems to mature, then prune lightly to keep in shape
Foliage Midgreen and long
Thorns Get out the gloves
As a cut flower Stunning; bring into the house and admire the petals, which are beautiful even as they drop
Similar varieties Honorine de Brabant; Commandant Beaurepaire

Excelsa

Like something out of a children's fairy story, this improbably perfect rose produces picture-perfect swathes of scarlet blooms. Great clusters of dark red buds erupt into a hot flow of crimson-red flowers that hang down from long stems and whose inner petals are flecked with white. The blooms fade to a dark pink as they age. The flowers are small, just 1¼ in (3 cm) in diameter and have little fragrance.

Let it rampage over walls, fences, arches and pergolas, and sit back and enjoy the show.

Excelsa, sometimes called Red Dorothy Perkins, was introduced by Michael Walsh in 1909. Walsh emigrated to the USA from North Wales in 1868 at the age of 20 and wound up as head gardener on a waterfront estate in Woods Hole, Cape Cod. He became a successful rose breeder, introducing around 40 new ramblers and taking awards both at home and abroad. This is a fabulous rose but it can be something of a martyr to mildew.

Flowering Late flowering but blooms once with a vengeance; there may be the odd repeat
Aspect Sunny but will tolerate partial shade
Soil Rich, moist and well drained but will tolerate most soils
Habit Vigorous rambler
Average height 158 in (4 m)
Average spread 79 in (2 m)
Pruning Prune to keep in check; it flowers on new stems
Foliage Glossy midgreen
Thorns Get the gloves out; it's vicious
As a cut flower Best enjoyed in the garden
Similar varieties Minnehaha (vigorous and a deep pink rather than red); Crimson Shower

Fighting Temeraire

David Austin (see p. 25) christened this rose in honor of the opening of the Turner Contemporary art gallery in Margate, Kent, in 2011. The connection to what is perhaps Turner's most famous painting, *The Fighting Temeraire*, is obvious at first glance – this rose is ablaze with the ever-changing colors of sunset. It buds a warm red, with its 10 petals opening to a warm flesh pink with sugar-pink tips. As it unfurls further, it reveals apricot-pink-edged petals that wash into a bright yellow at the base. As the flower matures, it pales subtly, the stamens becoming longer and more showily gold. The flowers can open to a diameter of around 5 in (12 cm) and have a strong, fruity fragrance with lemon overtones.

Fighting Temeraire is good at the middle or back of a mixed border.

Flowering Repeat-flowers
Aspect Sunny but will tolerate partial shade
Soil Rich, moist and well drained
Habit Vigorous, upright shrub
Average height 59 in (1.5 m)
Average spread 59 in (1.5 m)
Pruning Light for the first few years, then cut back by one-third
Foliage Dark green
Thorns Yes
As a cut flower Stunning, especially in a dark corner
Similar varieties Penelope (see p. 42); Morning Mist

Thomas à Becket

Liturgical in hue, it is perhaps not surprising that David Austin (see p. 25) selected this rose to honor Canterbury Cathedral. Thomas Becket, Archbishop of Canterbury from 1162, was murdered in Canterbury Cathedral by four of Henry II's knights on 11 December 1170. The knights had the mistaken belief that they were following the king's wishes. Becket was hailed a martyr and his tomb in Canterbury Cathedral became a place of pilgrimage. He was canonized in 1173 and his shrine still attracts hordes of visitors.

This rose, a sumptuous and bloody carmine red, is a multipetaled, shallow-cupped, rosette. The flowers, which open to 4 in (10 cm) in diameter, wave and nod in the breeze on relaxed stems, perfuming the air with a delicious Old-rose fragrance. The flowers are far from uptight but have a divertingly chaotic petal arrangement; there's no stiff formality here. Keep picking and deadheading to encourage more flowers to form. This shrub, introduced by Austin in 2015, can grow taller if left unpruned.

Thomas à Becket is pleasingly relaxed in character and blends well in a mixed border. It looks stunning with shades of purple and blue.

Flowering Repeat-flowers in summer
Aspect Sunny but will tolerate partial shade
Soil Rich, moist and well drained
Habit Shrub
Average height 48 in (1.2 m)
Average spread 35 in (90 cm)
Pruning Reduce height by one-half and streamline the interior architecture
Foliage Midgreen
Thorns Some
As a cut flower Spectacular
Similar varieties Tam O'Shanter

Lady of Shalott

Arthurian legend tells of Elaine of Astolat, who died of unrequited love for Sir Lancelot – he only had eyes for Queen Guinevere. She was immortalized by Alfred, Lord Tennyson's poem "The Lady of Shalott," published in 1833 and 1842. Tennyson depicts her weaving in a tower on the island of Shalott, cursed to only view the world through its reflection in a mirror. On sight of Lancelot in the mirror, she is entranced and turns to gaze at him through the window. She flees the tower, clambers into a boat – my words not Tennyson's – and dies en route to Camelot, thus becoming a tragic emblem of medieval purity.

David Austin (see p. 25) was asked to name a rose by The Tennyson Society to commemorate the 200th anniversary in 2009 of the poet's birth. Perhaps the autumnal palette of John William Waterhouse's famous painting *The Lady of Shalott* inspired Austin's choice of this glowing orange-red beauty.

Lady of Shalott's buds are yellow and coral and open into the most exquisite blooms. Austin describes them as "chalice-shaped" since the undersides of the petals are visible; I'd describe them as resembling a magnificent cross between a peony and a ranunculus. On closer inspection, the outside petals are apricot tinged with raspberry, while the inner petals are a warm, golden yellow. The overall effect is of a magnificent autumnal orange rose, with a luminous glow from within. The blooms, which open on twiggy stems to a diameter of 4 in (10 cm), have a good Tea-rose scent and subdue in tone as they mature.

This rose sits well in the middle or back of the border and is best mixed with hot color schemes – dark reds and rich purples.

Flowering Repeat-flowers
Aspect Sunny but will tolerate partial shade
Soil Rich, moist and well drained; feed regularly
Habit Bushy shrub
Average height 48 in (1.2 m)
Average spread 39 in (1 m)
Pruning Reduce in winter by one-third to one-half
Foliage Bronze when young, turning midgreen
Thorns Few
As a cut flower Magnificent alone or mixed with
other bright flowers
Similar varieties Lady Emma Hamilton

Boscobel

As a general rule, coral roses make me nervous. There is something about the flat rawness of the color that can dominate a flowerbed or planting scheme. Boscobel is the exception to my rule, for it glows with such a dramatic intensity and is a bloom of such superlative beauty that it cannot be denied. This rose is a couture beauty, with livid pink outer petals and flaming salmon-pink and coral-pink inner petals with the occasional flash of pale tangerine – an inspired clash of tones that lifts the spirits.

It buds a dark greenish purple and explodes into huge, luminous cupped tutus of flowers that are borne on long stems. These double rosettes spread to a diameter of 4 in (10 cm) and have a deliciously strong perfume.

In a border it looks splendid mixed with cool blues and purples. David Austin (see p. 25) introduced Boscobel in 2012. It is named after Boscobel House, where Charles II hid in an oak tree while attempting to evade Parliamentary soldiers on 6 September 1651. A descendant of the original tree now marks the spot.

Flowering Repeat-flowers
Aspect Sunny
Soil Rich, moist and well drained
Habit Shrub with tall, upright stems
Average height 35 in (90 cm)
Average spread 27½ in (70 cm)
Pruning Reduce by half in winter
Foliage Dark green and glossy
Thorns Some
As a cut flower Exceptional blooms on long stems
Similar varieties Jubilee Celebration

Boscobel

Anne Boleyn

Anne Boleyn has a breathtaking color palette. To describe it merely as a pink rose is to do it a grave injustice. The buds open a deep red pink, paling rapidly to a warm sugar pink and making a perfect rosette of petals, paler at the outer edges and warming in intensity to the heart. Here, some petals are a warm apricot with the odd dash of coral. These are the perfectly blended colors of a glorious pink sunset before the shades of violet creep in. Anne Boleyn flowers singly or in clusters of up to 10 blooms that can open to a diameter of 3½ in (9 cm). It has a light, sweet fragrance and when fully unfurled, reveals golden stamens at its heart.

This rose was introduced by David Austin (see p. 25) in 1999. It is named after Henry VIII's second wife, who took many illicit rose-garden walks with Henry before they were married – her badge was a white falcon alighting on roses. Anne was mother to Henry's second daughter, Princess Elizabeth, later Queen Elizabeth I. Henry's passion for Anne, once married, was short lived; he had her executed for adultery at the Tower of London on 2 May 1536. She was buried in an unmarked grave in the Chapel Royal of St. Peter ad Vincula. The grave was uncovered during restoration work in the nineteenth century and is now marked.

Flowering Repeat-flowers into autumn
Aspect Sunny
Soil Rich, moist and well drained
Habit Small, arching shrub
Average height 39 in (1 m)
Average spread 48 in (1.2 m)
Pruning Flowers on new wood, so prune in late winter to promote growth
Foliage Dark green
Thorns Yes
As a cut flower Prettily informal
Similar varieties Olivia Rose Austin (see p. 170); Gentle Hermione

Super Dorothy

It is the form of this descendant of Dorothy Perkins that gives it such dramatic visual impact. A lax dandy, it produces heavy sprays of up to 50 diminutive blooms that hang down in great pink floral swathes. It has tiny pale pink buds, which open to a ruffled and wayward mass of bright pink to midpink petals. The backs of the petals are paler in hue, and the blooms, which have virtually no perfume, fade through a range of pink tones with age. The flowers open to a diameter of 1½–2 in (4–5 cm).

Super Dorothy is a good rambler, resplendent on arches, pergolas and posts. The German rose grower Karl Hetzel introduced it in 1986.

Flowering Repeat-flowers through the summer and into autumn
Aspect Sunny
Soil Rich, moist and well drained
Habit Rambler
Average height 119 in (3 m)
Average spread 98 in (2.5 m)
Pruning Prune to keep in shape and tie in arching stems
Foliage Small, green and glossy
Thorns Yes
As a cut flower Lovely mixed in with other blooms
Similar varieties China Doll; Super Fairy

Blue for You

Despite its name, you can see for yourself that Blue for You is not really a true blue rose. Breeders have searched for one – the Holy Grail of rose growing – for centuries. There may be a blue rose in the not-too-distant future, but in the meantime Blue for You is as close as we get.

It is actually distinctly violet in hue, with long, plum-colored buds that open to a tight curl of violet petals. These unfurl again to a wavy frill of a bloom; the undulating petals carry veins of color, some with the occasional splash of white and all tipped with white at the base. The flower fades and grays as it ages so that it takes on more of a bluish tinge. It has a good scent, and when sniffing it you'll see dull gold stamens at its heart. This rose was introduced by Peter J. James in 2006 and took the Royal Horticultural Society's Award of Garden Merit in 2012.

Roses do not come in shades of blue because they lack the necessary pigmentation – delphinidin. The Japanese have been working on this, with the company Suntory having spent an enormous sum on the development of a blue rose – in excess of three billion yen! Applause, Suntory's first blue rose, was introduced in Japan in 2009 and in the USA in 2011, but in the USA, only as a cut flower for florists. But is Applause blue? Perhaps lavender would be a closer description. Speaking personally, I don't see the need for a blue rose.

Flowering Repeat-flowers
Aspect Sunny and sheltered
Soil Rich, moist and well drained
Habit Small shrub
Average height 32 in (80 cm)
Average spread 32 in (80 cm)
Pruning Not much needed
Foliage Midgreen and glossy
Thorns Few
As a cut flower Offsets other bright roses superbly
Similar varieties Rhapsody in Blue

Leonardo da Vinci

Leonardo da Vinci is an exceptionally pretty rose that just begs to be picked – the bush is positively laden with inviting pink posies of small, perfectly formed clusters. The buds are a raspberry pink, unfurling to reveal multipetaled, rosette-shaped cups of papery, sugar-pink petals that fade to a pale pink. When the buds are fully open, you can glimpse a tiny yellow eye peeking out from the profusion of curling petals, each with a green-white splash at its base. Leonardo da Vinci is lightly fragranced.

Unlike many roses, this one has great tolerance to rain, which is a huge plus – it's hard not to be downcast by a beautiful array of rose blooms being spoiled by a heavy downpour. It does best in a warm, sunny position, where it can grow into a small climber.

Leonardo da Vinci (aka Léonard da Vinci) was introduced by the French rose grower Meilland in 1994.

Flowering Repeat-flowers during summer
Aspect Sunny
Soil Rich, moist and well drained
Habit Bushy shrub
Average height 48 in (1.2 m)
Average spread 39 in (1 m)
Pruning It flowers on new wood, so cut out some old wood each spring to promote flowering
Foliage Glossy green
Thorns A plethora of red thorns
As a cut flower Stunning and mixes well with other colors
Similar varieties Lady Meilland

Magenta with Blue for You (see p. 124)

Magenta

Yet another rose that doesn't quite color-match its name! Its blooms are a superb faded violet combined with a grayed pink, like faded pink paper roses. The color is superb and even more artful as the blooms fade and mature. The buds are a true, rich magenta but open into a ruffled petticoat of a bloom – a wanton, loose rosette of disorganized petals that spread to a diameter of 2¾ in (7 cm). It buds in generous flusters of 5–15 flowers that have a strong fragrance. At their heart is a cluster of golden yellow stamens.

The lower stems of this rose can be rather bare so it works well as part of a mixed border, where you can conceal its ankles with other herbaceous plants. Magenta is simply glorious in arrangements, solo or mixed. Let the petals drop where they will – the whole effect is entrancing.

Magenta was introduced in 1954 by the creative German rose breeder Wilhelm Kordes II. I don't usually mention parentage but in this instance it is worth checking out one-half of Magenta's gene pool – a rose called Lavender Pinocchio, a great overblown beauty with flowers the color of fudge that fade to a lavender pink.

Flowering Repeat-flowers in bursts until midautumn
Aspect Sunny
Soil Rich, moist and well drained
Habit Open shrub
Average height 59 in (1.5 m)
Average spread 49 in (1.25 m)
Pruning Can grow taller if only lightly pruned
Foliage Dark green
Thorns Reddish prickles
As a cut flower Superb color for flower arranging
Similar varieties Blue Magenta (a darker Floribunda rambler)

Rosarium Uetersen

This is an attention-seeking rose that is a sight to behold when in full flower. It has had the misfortune to be dubbed coral pink by many rose growers but in reality it is a bold, blowsy pink. I'll grant you that Rosarium Uetersen buds a coral pink but it opens to a ruffled mass of orange-pink petals, the undersides of which are rather paler. The blooms appear in great swathes across the plant, reaching 3½ in (9 cm) in diameter and emitting a sweet fragrance. The flowers age prettily so the whole effect is a glowing mass of graded pink magnificence – like throwing open the doors of Barbara Cartland's wardrobe.

Reimer Kordes introduced this rose in 1977. It was named after the north German rose garden in Uetersen that is home to over 800 varieties of rose and which the Kordes nursery helped to create in 1934.

Flowering First huge flush in early summer, then repeat-flowers intermittently
Aspect Sunny
Soil Rich, moist and well drained
Habit Climber
Average height 138 in (3.5 m)
Average spread 98 in (2.5 m)
Pruning Attack in winter, removing dead and diseased growth; cut back side shoots and tie in new shoots
Foliage Midgreen
Thorns Some
As a cut flower Cut armfuls and dot around the house
Similar varieties St. Swithun Climbing rose (much softer pink in tone); Strawberry Hill

Wild Blue Yonder

This vibrant Floribunda rose, faintly reminiscent of a camellia in form, has rich purplish blooms – though it can photograph as a pinkish red – and a heady rose-and-citrus perfume. It has fat, pointed purple buds that open to a ruffle of 25–30 petals, each tipped lavender at the base and with a heart of golden stamens. It blooms in generous clusters on long stems, and the flowers, which can reach 3 in (8 cm) in diameter, fade to lavender as they age. It is variable, being deeper and darker in tone in cooler temperatures. This is a hungry plant that benefits from regular feeding and a very sunny position.

Wild Blue Yonder was introduced by the award-winning Texas rose hybridizer Tom Carruth in 2006, and it took the All-America Rose Selections Award the same year – the first time a lavender-hued bloom had won in over 20 years. Tom Carruth is, at the time of writing, working as curator of the Rose Garden at The Huntington Library and Botanical Gardens in Southern California.

Flowering Repeat-flowers
Aspect Sunny
Soil Rich, moist and well drained
Habit Long-stemmed, upright shrub
Average height 59 in (1.5 m)
Average spread 48 in (1.2 m)
Pruning Cut out dead and diseased wood in early spring
Foliage Dark green and glossy
Thorns Yes
As a cut flower Exquisite color – even the dropping petals retain their color
Similar varieties Roseraie de l'Hay (similar in color though not in form)

ROMANTIC
BEAUTIES

Legend has it that when the Greek goddess Aphrodite – Venus to the Romans – sprang from the waves, the Earth, not to be outdone, created the rose to equal the beauty of the goddess. Now roses are so weighted with centuries of romantic symbolism that they have become something of a Valentine's Day cliché – some 110 million roses are sold on Valentine's Day in the USA annually, and the figure rises with every year that passes. It is ironic that red roses have become the most romantic symbol of all; they do not occur in nature but have only been developed through breeding. The first true red rose didn't appear until the late eighteenth century and red roses are still prone to weak necks even after all this time. Undoubtedly the fragrance of the rose has something to do with its allure – our olfactory receptors are connected to the limbic system, the most primitive part of the brain and one that is linked to our emotions. Here we offer a selection of the prettiest roses – soft, inviting, fragrant and guaranteed to generate emotion. Like people, they come in a range of characters, moods and coloratura.

A Shropshire Lad

Winner of the Royal Horticultural Society's Award of Garden Merit in 2012,
A Shropshire Lad was introduced by David Austin (see p. 25) – a Shropshire
lad himself – in 1996.

It has coral-pink buds opening to soft, peachy pink flowers. Their smaller central
petals are warm in tone, fading to a pale shell pink on the outer petals, which are
paler still at their tips. It is blessed with a strong, fruity, Tea-rose perfume and blooms
in clusters of 3–10 flowers, which, if properly pruned, will appear from the base of
the plant to the top.

Flowering Repeat-flowers from late spring until the first frosts
Aspect Sunny but will tolerate partial shade
Soil Rich, fertile and well drained
Habit Large shrub or good climber
Average height 59–98 in (1.5–2.5 m)
Average spread 59 in (1.5 m)
Pruning Remove some old wood and shorten the side shoots
Foliage Dark green and glossy
Thorns Few
As a cut flower Good for relaxed, informal arrangements
Similar varieties James Galway (see p. 166)

Félicité-Perpétue

Rose grower Antoine Jacques, head gardener to the Duc d'Orléans, named his roses to honor his esteemed employer – with one exception. When Jacques' wife was pregnant, he determined to name his next rose after his child. The arrival of twin girls on 7 March 1827 presented him with a dilemma: how to incorporate both names? Since 7 March was the feast day of the third-century Christian martyrs Félicité and Perpétue, one a noblewoman and the other a slave, mauled to death by wild animals in a Carthaginian amphitheater, Jacques named his twin girls after them. He then combined the two names to use for his rose. Félicité-Perpétue remains a firm favorite thanks to its exceptional beauty and reliability.

This vigorous Sempervirens rambler has deep pink-red buds that open to a creamy pinkish white, fading to white. Each rose is a powder-puff rosette of perfect petals with a green eye at its heart. The fragrance is lovely and light. Félicité-Perpétue erupts in great abundant clusters of 20–40 flowers and in season it is smothered in blooms. Its only drawback is a tendency to keep a tenacious grip on its petals so that as the flowers fade, they brown on the plant.

Also known as Félicité et Perpétue, this rose is best planted where it can ramble unchecked – so grow it over a garage or a tree stump. Courtesy of New York florist Peter Henderson, we have a popular mutation, or sport, White Pet, that was introduced in 1879. This smaller evergreen shrub blooms continually, though like Félicité-Perpétue, it hangs onto its fading petals.

Flowering Once in midsummer
Aspect Very tolerant; it will even survive shade
Soil Likes a fertile soil and responds to regular feeding
Habit Vigorous rambler
Average height 200 in (5 m)
Average spread 119 in (3 m)
Pruning Let it run riot; pruning will discourage flowering and simply promote more growth
Foliage Dark red plum color when young, turning green and glossy
As a cut flower Lovely clusters for informal arrangements
Similar varieties Princesse Louise

Félicité Parmentier

The nineteenth-century Belgian Louis-Joseph Ghislaine Parmentier was a prolific rose grower. What started as a hobby grew into a grand obsession – he bred over 800 varieties in his lifetime. Some of these are the ancestors of our most popular modern roses.

The precise origins of this particular rose are lost in time, though we know it was first introduced in 1828 and is thought to be a hybrid between an Alba and a Damask rose. Its longevity lies in its exceptionally beautiful flowers that simply beg to be cut. The flat, scented blooms are a cupped, multipetaled extravagance, with a button eye at the center. The buds are fleshy yellow green, changing to a fleshy pink, then fading from pale pink to white as the bloom matures, with exquisite grades of harmonizing tones in between. The flowers are smallish, 2–2¾ in (5–7 cm) in diameter, but they grow in profuse clusters of 3–8. The bush flowers for 6–8 weeks.

Despite its fragile beauty, this plant is quite sturdy and can be used in hedges but it does need some sunshine to flower. It relishes a mulch of humus-rich soil every year and will thank you for an annual helping of manure. It enjoys an annual pruning; cut the height down by one-third each year but only give it a light prune to begin with.

Flowering One long, single flowering in midsummer
Aspect Sunny but will tolerate partial shade
Soil Moist and well drained
Habit Stiff, upright growth
Average height 39 in (1 m)
Average spread 39 in (1 m)
Pruning Light
Foliage Gray green
Thorns Moderately thorny
As a cut flower Gorgeous
Similar varieties Gloire des Mousseux; Queen of Denmark

Rambling Rector

The true origins of this rose, which is thought to date back to the nineteenth century, are unknown but it is quite a sight in full flower. It is for this reason that it took the Royal Horticultural Society's Award of Garden Merit in 1993.

It will clamber over or through anything and is perfect as a screen for unsightly garden buildings. In midsummer it will produce cream buds that open to charming, diminutive, creamy white flowers, which fade to white. The double-petaled flowers have masses of golden yellow stamens at their heart and are produced in generous clusters of 10–50 blooms, each flower measuring just 1½ in (4 cm) in diameter. The flowers have a strong, musky perfume. The whole plant is festooned and swathed in flowers like some artful florist's display. Even the hard-hearted will find it difficult to resist this plant's romantic allure. After flowering, Rambling Rector produces masses of small orange rose hips.

This vigorous plant will scramble away with great speed but the young shoots are soft and pliable, and easy to train. Theoretically you can keep it pruned as a large shrub but it takes a lot of pruning to keep it under control; it's better to let it have its head and run wild.

Flowering Once in midsummer from June to July
Aspect Sunny
Soil Well drained and moist; mulch in spring with compost or well-rotted manure
Habit Rampant rambler
Average height 138 in (3.5 m)
Average spread 79 in (2 m)
Pruning Remove one-third of the old stems annually in late summer to promote healthy new growth, and cut the side shoots back by two-thirds
Foliage Pale green
Thorns Wear gloves for pruning
As a cut flower Use the long stems in arching arrangements
Similar varieties Filipes 'Kiftsgate'; Adélaïde d'Orléans

Ballerina

Its flowers may be small but Ballerina took the Royal Horticultural Society's Award of Garden Merit in 1993. Its attraction is that it produces clusters of delicate, simple, pale pink flowers, with a splash of white at the base. In the center is a halo of golden stamens. The buds are a raspberry pink with pale green sepals that protrude at right angles. The clusters of flowers get bigger and more magnificent as the season progresses and it will keep on flowering until the first frosts – long after most other roses have ceased to put on a show. The flowers can bleach as they age, so each cluster is a harmonious assortment of pink and white blooms.

This Hybrid Musk was introduced by Jack Bentall in 1937. He learned his craft working for the esteemed rose fancier Reverend Joseph Hardwick Pemberton (see p. 21). Aside from being planted in the border, Ballerina can make a useful hedge as well as flourishing in pots. It can also be sculpted into a Standard rose, though I am of the firm opinion that neither roses nor poodles are natural subjects for topiary.

Flowering Late but continual

Aspect Sunny but will tolerate partial shade

Soil Rich, moist and well drained

Habit Dense, spreading shrub

Average height 59 in (1.5 m)

Average spread 59 in (1.5 m)

Pruning In the border, give it its head; otherwise prune to shape

Foliage Midgreen

Thorns Yes, large

As a cut flower Best enjoyed in the garden

Similar varieties Jacqueline du Pré (white and semidouble)

Kew Rambler, with flowers closely resembling those of Ballerina, is a vigorous climber and perfect for a pergola or arbor

Tranquillity

As contemporary paint charts show, there is no such color as plain white; Tranquillity is the perfect example of a warm, multitoned "white" rose. It buds a raspberry green, unfurling to creamy pink perfection, then unfolding further to reveal hints of creamy yellow at its heart. The blooms are a positive profusion of petals that form a fulsome rosette, some 4 in (10 cm) in diameter, and exude a light, apple fragrance. This rose is lovely in a mixed border and looks superb with shades of pink and lavender. Prune it to suit its situation; it can grow quite tall given half a chance.

Launched in 2014 by David Austin (see p. 25), it was named to reflect the tranquil nature of its soft white hues.

Flowering Repeat-flowers
Aspect Sunny
Soil Tolerates poor soil
Habit Bushy, upright shrub
Average height 48 in (1.2 m)
Average spread 35 in (90 cm)
Pruning Cut down by one-third to two-thirds in winter
Foliage Light green
Thorns Blessedly few
As a cut flower Stunning cut flowers but not long lived
Similar varieties Winchester Cathedral (see p. 201); Crocus Rose

Vanity

If ever a rose was misnamed, this is it, for aside from its rich, sugar-pink color, it is quite a modest rose. Its breeder, the Reverend Joseph Hardwick Pemberton (see p. 21), who introduced it in 1920, obviously thought otherwise.

The buds are a dark, deep pink and the simple flowers have a double layer of warm pink, curling, pleated petals, tipped white at their base, that fade with age. The blooms unfurl to 2¾ in (7 cm) in diameter and reveal an artful circlet of thick yellow stamens that are loved by bees. The flowers are followed by orange hips. This Hybrid Musk rose has a good, musky perfume.

Vanity is sometimes criticized for its unprepossessing foliage – it's a bit on the thin side – but the flowers, which seem to bloom almost continuously, make it a splendid plant for the back of the border. A group clustered together makes a somewhat glowing impact. As Vanity has a rather hot-pink hue, it can dominate some color schemes but mixes well with blues, purples and violets, both in the flower bed and in the vase.

Flowering Repeat-flowers
Aspect Tolerates a little shade
Soil Moist and well drained
Habit Arching shrub
Average height 79 in (2 m)
Average spread 59 in (1.5 m)
Pruning Cut back by about one-third
Foliage Dark green and rather sparse
Thorns Some
As a cut flower Pretty in mixed cottage-garden arrangements
Similar varieties Nur Mahal (a bolder pink red with white flashes); The Lady's Blush

Grace

Budding an intense and vibrant coppery yellow, Grace unfurls into a froufrou vision of apricot frilliness, with all the subtlety of shade and tone of a still-life painting. Intense, but never vulgar, the color is strongest at the heart of the bloom, paling and fading in hue to the outer petals and bleaching further with maturity. It's hard to pick a bunch of these flowers, which bloom in nodding rosettes, and achieve anything other than a stunningly relaxed, warm arrangement.

Grace is charming in a mixed border and can be pruned to curtail or celebrate its arching habit. Either cut it back by two-thirds annually or restrict yourself to a mere light trim, but do not fail to remove dead, diseased or crossing growth. The fully double, cupped blooms, which reach a diameter of around 3½ in (9 cm), have a lovely warm fragrance.

Launched in 2001 by David Austin (see p. 25), Grace was awarded the Royal Horticultural Society's Award of Garden Merit in 2012. It was named to celebrate the particular grace of Austin's English Roses as a group.

Flowering Repeat-flowers

Aspect Sunny

Soil Tolerates poor soil

Habit Medium-sized arching shrub

Average height 41 in (105 cm)

Average spread 48 in (1.2 m)

Pruning Light or cut back by two-thirds, depending on desired shape

Foliage Midgreen

Thorns Yes

As a cut flower Exquisite drooping blooms, stunning alone or mixed with reds and purples

Similar varieties Port Sunlight

Queen of Sweden

Roses don't come much more romantic than this in appearance. The flowers, though small – around 2¾ in (7 cm) in diameter – are exceptionally beautiful. Each has an exquisite perfection and they keep on coming in small clusters. The coppery pink buds open to produce apricot-pink flowers, fading to palest pale pink around the exterior petals. Each flower is shallow and forms cupped rosettes. It has a pleasing but light myrrh fragrance.

This English Musk hybrid was introduced by David Austin (see p. 25) in 2004 and is a cross between an Old rose and a Noisette. It makes a charming cut flower and will drop its petals prettily. Austin named it to commemorate 350 years of friendship between Sweden and Great Britain.

Flowering Late spring onwards; it can repeat-flower until the first frosts
Aspect Sunny
Soil Light, fertile and well drained
Habit Upright, bushy shrub
Average height 48 in (1.2 m)
Average spread 29 in (75 cm)
Pruning Reduce in winter by one-third to one-half
Foliage Dark green
Thorns Few
As a cut flower Excellent
Similar varieties Scepter'd Isle

Kathryn Morley

Rose lovers grow this species for the exceptional beauty of its flowers. The yellow buds blush to a deep pink at their tips and open to cupped, multipetaled flowers of a sweet, soft pink. The petals are paler at the tips and fade with age. The flowers, around 3½ in (9 cm) in diameter, are borne in small clusters and come in many forms – an eruption of curling petals, full and double or quartered, with a tiny visible golden eye. The color remains strongest at the heart of the flower. Kathryn Morley also boasts a strong, sweet Tea-rose fragrance.

Introduced by David Austin (see p. 25) in 1990, the shrub is prone to powdery mildew in cool, damp areas but thrives in warm climates, where it can grow far beyond its average size.

The name was auctioned at a charity event and purchased by Eric and Julia Morley in memory of their daughter Kathryn, who died aged 17. The flower is a true salute to her.

Flowering Repeat-flowers
Aspect Sunny
Soil Rich, moist and well drained
Habit Bushy, upright shrub
Average height 55 in (1.4 m)
Average spread 39 in (1 m)
Pruning Flowers on new wood; prune out old wood to encourage flowering
Foliage Dark green and large
Thorns Get the gloves out; this shrub has large thorns
As a cut flower Informal
Similar varieties St. Swithun

Mon Jardin et Ma Maison

This is a sugar-coated cupcake of a rose, with a colorist's exquisite subtlety of tone. The long, pale pink buds begin to open to creamy flowers with a suggestion of warm buttery pink at the center. As they continue to unfurl, they reveal a soft shell-pink interior, sometimes with a hint of a tangerine cream, too, all finished off with a sunburst of bright yellow stamens at the heart. This rose looks as though it is lit from within and is exceptionally lovely. As it matures, it turns to soft white and the petals acquire hints of pale lemon. At a distance you could mistake it for a good white Old rose but it deserves close examination. It is nothing short of a multipetaled extravaganza of a rose. The flowers come singly or in clusters of up to six and reach a diameter of around 4 in (10 cm). It has a sweet, light perfume.

Plant it near to the house so you can admire its beauty close up. Leave it alone, apart from training, for a few years. Bring the blooms into your home and admire its perfection from bud to dropping flower, either solo, or arranged with other pink, peach and white roses.

Mon Jardin et Ma Maison was suitably named for the French lifestyle magazine of the same name. The rose grower, Meilland Richardier, introduced it in 1998.

Flowering Repeat-flowers
Aspect Sunny
Soil Rich, moist and well drained
Habit Climber
Average height 79 in (2 m)
Average spread 39 in (1 m)
Pruning Shape as required and remove some old wood
Foliage Glossy green
Thorns Few
As a cut flower Heavenly
Similar varieties The Generous Gardener

James Galway

This confection of a rose has dark pink buds that open to multipetaled flowers, which darken from the pale outer tips of their petals to their warm, sugar-pink heart. The large, fulsome and frilly blooms have great whorls of perfectly placed petals. With their delicious Old-rose fragrance, the blooms just beg to be sniffed.

This tall shrub sits beautifully at the back of a border and blends very amicably with other garden flowers. It is blissfully thorn free, making the business of pruning much less of a chore. If you give it its head, it will happily grow to a small climber.

James Galway was introduced by David Austin (see p. 25) in 2000 and was named in honor of world-famous Irish flautist James Galway to commemorate his 60th birthday.

Flowering Repeat-flowers from late spring until the first frosts
Aspect Will tolerate shade
Soil Moist and well drained
Habit Arching shrub or small climber
Average height 59–98 in (1.5–2.5 m)
Average spread 39 in (1 m)
Pruning Reduce height of shrubs by one-third in winter; reduce climber's side shoots to 3–4 buds
Foliage Rich green
Thorns Few
As a cut flower Relaxed and informal
Similar varieties A Shropshire Lad (see p. 138)

Buttercup

The apricot buds of this pretty rose open their long, feathery sepals to reveal buttercup-yellow, cupped, semidouble blooms. These fade slightly with age but retain their wonderfully sunny tone. The petals unfurl right back to reveal a corona of sulfur-yellow stamens. The flowers, which have a light Tea-rose fragrance, are superb in a vase, will brighten any corner to spectacular effect and are perfect mixed with other brights.

The plant is light and airy and the clusters of flowers are borne in a perfect display on tall, arching stems. It does not do well in shade but is happy in a sunny border or in a container. Buttercup was introduced by David Austin (see p. 25) in 1998. The name celebrates its resemblance to the wild buttercup in color and habit.

Flowering Repeat-flowers

Aspect Sunny

Soil Rich, moist and well drained but tolerant of most soil types

Habit Tall and upright

Average height 48 in (1.2 m)

Average spread 39 in (1 m)

Pruning In winter reduce height by one-third to one-half

Foliage Light green

Thorns Yes

As a cut flower A gorgeous cut flower with pretty foliage on long stems

Similar varieties Thisbe; Callisto

Olivia Rose Austin

This perfectly pink rose is a 2014 introduction from David Austin (see p. 25) and was named after the rose grower's granddaughter. The flowers are formed in best Old-rose tradition; the buds are a warm pink, fading as they open to a sugary-pink sweetness of multipetaled rosettes that pleat out from a barely visible golden eye. The flowers will reach 3½ in (9 cm) in diameter and have a fruity fragrance with hints of plum.

It blooms early in the season and sheds its petals prettily, which ensures that the blooms look as good in the border as they do in small, informal arrangements.

Flowering Repeat-flowers late spring to autumn
Aspect Sunny
Soil Rich, moist and well drained
Habit Shrub
Average height 35 in (90 cm)
Average spread 29 in (75 cm)
Pruning Light pruning for its first few years, then cut back by one- to two-thirds
Foliage Glossy green
Thorns Few
As a cut flower Perfect in a small bottle or jam jar when you want early blooms indoors
Similar varieties The Ancient Mariner

Tradescant

This sensuous wine-red Gothic beauty buds a deep, dark red, unfurling to shallow-cupped blooms with quilled and quartered petals that pale as they age and retract further still into a can-can dancer's seductive tutu. The blooms, which reach around 3 in (8 cm) in diameter, have a deliciously strong, rich perfume. These exquisite blooms, which come in clusters of 5–10, simply beg to be picked.

The downside – or upside depending on where you live – is that Tradescant performs best only in hot climates such as California and Australia, where it can be grown as a small climber, reaching around 95 in (2.4 m) in height. In temperate climates it is more likely to struggle. It does suffer somewhat from black spot and rust. Tradescant benefits from a good feeding regime. David Austin (see p. 25) introduced this rose in 1994.

Flowering Repeat-flowers
Aspect Sunny
Soil Rich, moist and well drained
Habit Arching shrub
Average height 48 in (1.2 m)
Average spread 48 in (1.2 m)
Pruning Light initially, then reduce by one-third
Foliage Midgreen
Thorns: Some
As a cut flower Intoxicating clusters; stupendous with blues, pinks and hot colors
Similar varieties William Shakespeare (fine in temperate climates); Munstead Wood

Alan Titchmarsh

More peony-like than a peony, this magnificent rose has great cupped blooms of nodding heads and a strong Old-rose fragrance that drifts on the air. The plant has fat pink buds that open to whorls of crisp, incurving, multipetaled extravagances. The outer petals are paler and darken to a soft or warm pink heart. In a vase they cannot help but resemble a still life by an Old Master.

This shrub is beautiful in the garden as part of a border. Pruned regularly, it will stay small but you can leave it to grow taller in the back of the bed.

Introduced by David Austin (see p. 25) in 2005 and named after the popular British horticulturalist Alan Titchmarsh, it is known in the USA as the Huntington Rose, having been named after the Huntington Library in San Marino, California – home to an important rose garden. That garden was designed, in part, for Arabella Huntington – once known as the richest woman in America – so she could utilize the cut blooms in elaborate floral arrangements.

Flowering Repeat-flowers
Aspect Sunny
Soil Rich, moist and well drained; mulch in spring
Habit Arching, rounded shrub
Average height 48 in (1.2 m)
Average spread 35 in (90 cm)
Pruning Cut stems back by one-half to keep the shrub compact or prune more lightly to allow it to grow taller
Foliage Red when young, turning green and glossy
Thorns Average
As a cut flower Short lived but glorious; sheds its petals quickly
Similar varieties The Alnwick

Alan Titchmarsh with Mary Rose

Jubilee Celebration

David Austin (see p. 25) describes this rose – introduced and named in honor of Queen Elizabeth II's Golden Jubilee in 2002 – as salmon pink. The perception of color is always open to personal interpretation, but in my book this is a much more interesting, warm, rich and intense shade of pink than the pink of the lurid-hued smoked fish.

The buds are a warm coppery yellow and it is this tint that gives the pink petals a deep, raspberry-sherbet intensity when they are open. The folded and pleated petals whorl around in an origami of domed sculptural perfection. The bush holds its flowers high, making a lovely showy display. Jubilee Celebration enjoys a superb perfume – a strong, fruity rose scent combined with a lemony zing and a diverting hint of raspberry.

Flowering Repeat-flowers
Aspect Sunny
Soil Rich, moist and well drained
Habit Bushy, arching shrub
Average height 48 in (1.2 m)
Average spread 48 in (1.2 m)
Pruning Reduce size by one- to two-thirds in winter and prune out dead and diseased wood
Foliage Dark green and plentiful
Thorns Quite thorny
As a cut flower Scents the air and looks lovely mixed with dark blue or purple blooms
Similar varieties Boscobel (see p. 114); Princess Anne

Yves Piaget

This multi-award-winning rose has whopping, sweet-scented, peony-like flowers –
so perfect that even home guru Martha Stewart favors them as cut flowers.

The buds are pale pink but darker at the tip and open into mighty blooms that reach
5 in (12 cm) in diameter. The petals are curled, furled and ruffled at the tips, with
a darker raspberry hue in the center paling to pale pink on the outer petals. As the
blooms fade, they pale and sometimes take on a lavender tint. Some petals in the heart
of the flower are flecked with white. Yves Piaget has a strong, sweet, fruity perfume
that readily scents the air. It is an exceptional flower for wedding bouquets and
arrangements, and looks stunning combined with shades of pale pink, green and blue.

This rose was introduced by Marie-Louise Meilland in 1985 and is one of Meilland
International's Romantica collection. It is named after Yves Piaget, the Swiss luxury
watchmaker.

Flowering Repeat-flowers from May until the first frosts
Aspect Sunny
Soil Rich, moist and well drained
Habit Upright bush
Average height 29 in (75 cm)
Average spread 20 in (50 cm)
Pruning Cut back after flowering by one-third to one-half
Foliage Glossy green and serrated
Thorns Yes
As a cut flower Long-lasting, scented flowers on long stems
Similar varieties St. Cecilia; Brother Cadfael

Tasogare

A sugary, sweet-pea lavender in hue, Tasogare is a Japanese rose introduced by Moriji Kobayashi in 1977. It is a dainty, frilled petticoat of a rose, with a delicate fluting of ruffled petals and a thicket of sulfur-yellow stamens at its heart. The buds are uncompromisingly purple. The flowers, which reach around 2¾ in (7 cm) in diameter, are not especially fragrant.

It blooms in flushes, which are strongest in late spring. Deadheading will promote repeat-flowering.

Tasogare means "sundown time" in Japanese, and is also used as a metaphor for old age.

Flowering Repeat-flowers in flushes
Aspect Sunny
Soil Rich, moist and well drained
Habit Small shrub
Average height 39 in (1 m)
Average spread 39 in (1 m)
Pruning Cut back old wood by one-quarter
Foliage Gray green
Thorns Some
As a cut flower Best enjoyed in the garden
Similar varieties Blueberry Hill; Clair Matin (more pink)

Amanogawa

This rose bears single, sulfur-yellow blooms on slender stems; the petals wave with age and fade to white at the tip. It blooms in clusters of 2–3 flowers, which reach around 2¾ in (7 cm) in diameter. Look inside and you'll see a bright red pistil. Amanogawa has a light fragrance and a delicate form that the Japanese adore, but this rose is less well known in Europe and the Americas.

The growth is arching and the rose is prone to powdery mildew and black spot. Amanogawa means "Milky Way" in Japanese. It was introduced by the Japanese rose grower Mr. Seizo Suzuki in 1963.

Flowering Repeat-flowers in flushes into autumn
Aspect Sunny
Soil Rich, moist and well drained
Habit Spreading
Average height 32 in (80 cm)
Average spread 32 in (80 cm)
Pruning Cut back by one-quarter in winter
Foliage Deep green
Thorns Yes
As a cut flower Best enjoyed in the garden
Similar varieties Darlow's Enigma

Garasha

Hosokawa Garasha was a Japanese samurai, daughter of a general and wife of a famous samurai warrior, who became a Christian convert. This semidouble palest pink rose, named in tribute to her, bears large, almost conical flowers that bloom from early summer into autumn.

Deadhead but leave the flowers in place late in the season if you want to encourage the production of rose hips. It has a graceful, spreading habit, with the blooms borne on slender stems in great flushes.

Flowering Repeat-flowers
Aspect Sunny
Soil Rich, moist and well drained
Habit Small, spreading shrub
Average height 79 in (2 m)
Average spread 79 in (2 m)
Pruning Light
Foliage Deep green
Thorns Yes
As a cut flower Best enjoyed in the garden
Similar varieties Cassie; Sally Holmes (see p. 80)

Pheasant

Though it blooms but once a season, Pheasant makes quite an impact. It erupts into a great mass of ruffled, untidy blooms long after most roses have finished flowering. The flowers, sometimes unkindly described as coral pink, appear in arched clusters of 10–30 nodding heads. It buds a warm pink, fading as it opens, and ages to a flesh pink. When the frilly petals unfurl fully, the blooms reach 2 in (5 cm) in diameter and you'll find a thatch of golden stamens at their heart. It has a light, musky perfume.

This shrub is happy to ramble and will obligingly rampage over small walls, but it is also amenable to training. It was initially developed for ground cover but is determined to oblige in all kinds of situations. The stems are supple so it is easy – though prickly – to train.

Pheasant was introduced by the German breeder Kordes in 1985. It is also known as Heidekönigin.

Flowering Once, late
Aspect Sunny
Soil Rich, moist and well drained
Habit Climber
Average height 39–79 in (1–2 m)
Average spread 79 in (2 m)
Pruning To shape
Foliage Dark and evergreen
Thorns Get the gloves out
As a cut flower Lovely in relaxed solo arrangements
Similar varieties Pink Cloud

FRAGRANT
DELIGHTS

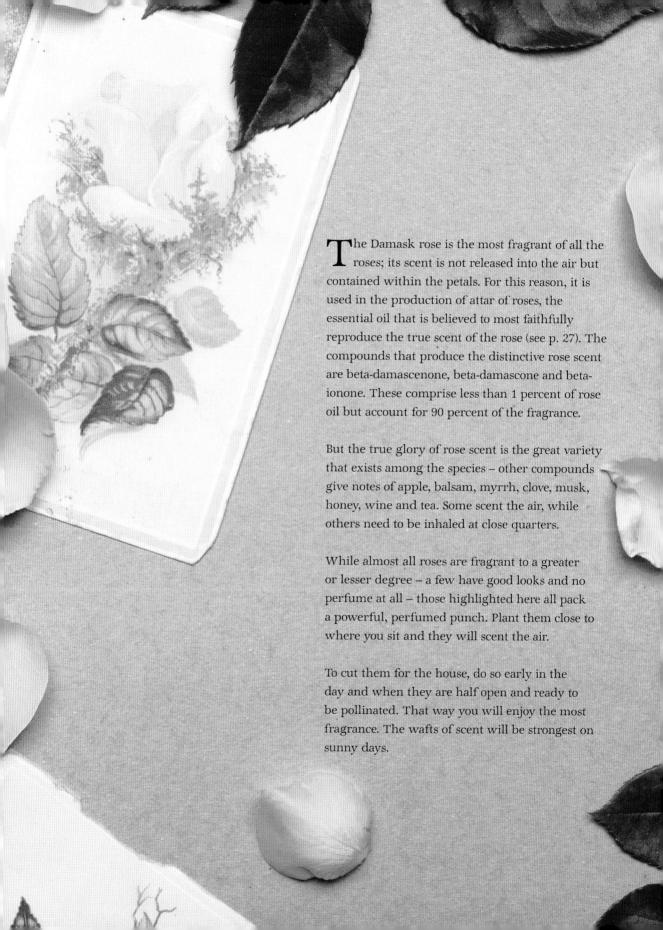

The Damask rose is the most fragrant of all the roses; its scent is not released into the air but contained within the petals. For this reason, it is used in the production of attar of roses, the essential oil that is believed to most faithfully reproduce the true scent of the rose (see p. 27). The compounds that produce the distinctive rose scent are beta-damascenone, beta-damascone and beta-ionone. These comprise less than 1 percent of rose oil but account for 90 percent of the fragrance.

But the true glory of rose scent is the great variety that exists among the species – other compounds give notes of apple, balsam, myrrh, clove, musk, honey, wine and tea. Some scent the air, while others need to be inhaled at close quarters.

While almost all roses are fragrant to a greater or lesser degree – a few have good looks and no perfume at all – those highlighted here all pack a powerful, perfumed punch. Plant them close to where you sit and they will scent the air.

To cut them for the house, do so early in the day and when they are half open and ready to be pollinated. That way you will enjoy the most fragrance. The wafts of scent will be strongest on sunny days.

Gertrude Jekyll

The exquisite planting schemes of the inspirational and influential English garden designer Gertrude Jekyll (see p. 21) earned her an international reputation and won her many awards. David Austin (see p. 25) introduced a rose named in her honor in 1986; it has since gone on to become one of the most popular roses in his collection.

Apart from being a rose of great beauty, Gertrude Jekyll is deservedly famous for its exceptional perfume; the blooms exude an intensely powerful Old-rose fragrance. The small, dark pink buds open with a speedy flourish into fulsome, dusky pink rosettes but this demure rose attempts to conceal its sepals underneath an artfully pleated spiral of petals. The flowers open to an impressive diameter of 4½ in (11 cm).

This vigorous shrub can be trained as a climber against a wall and will grow taller in warm climates. Just make sure you plant it near the house, where the fragrance can float in through open windows, or against a pergola you like to sit beneath, so you can breathe in the heady perfume. It needs to be deadheaded and pruned lightly through the summer to keep the flowers coming. Often, things of such beauty have to have one flaw – and in the case of Gertrude Jekyll it is her rather vicious array of thorns. Wear gloves; she scratches!

Gertrude Jekyll took the Royal Horticultural Society's Award of Garden Merit in 1994. It was voted Britain's favorite flower in the BBC television's *Gardeners' World* poll in 2006.

Flowering Repeat-flowers
Aspect Sunny but will tolerate partial shade
Soil Rich, moist and well drained
Habit Shrub or climber
Average height 59 in (1.5 m)
Average spread 48 in (1.2 m)
Pruning Reduce shrubs by one- to two-thirds in winter; reduce climber's side shoots to 3–4 buds
Foliage Gray green
Thorns Get the gloves out; this rose is vicious
As a cut flower Beautiful and fragrant; some blooms grow on long stems
Similar varieties Jubilee Celebration; Princess Alexandra of Kent

Winchester Cathedral

All roses are beautiful but Winchester Cathedral has the full package – beauty and fragrance. It buds a mix of raspberry cream and green that fades to the palest shell pink as it begins to unfurl, fading further as it opens into a frilly white ruff of a rose. The petals are cupped initially, then reflex to reveal curls of inner petals and occasionally the merest hint of gold stamens. The flowers, which reach around 4 in (10 cm) in diameter, are borne on long, thorny stems, which are the only downside. The blooms have a glorious fragrance – a honeyed Old rose with notes of almond blossom.

This is a superb garden shrub that is splendid as part of a mixed border; the blooms also make exceptional flowers for cutting. It is a sport of David Austin's (see p. 25) Mary Rose and sometimes reverts back to its parent, but this is almost a bonus, as it then produces the odd flower, or stem, of pink blooms.

David Austin introduced this rose in 1998; it was named to mark Winchester Cathedral's 900th year. The cathedral has a history dating back to the seventh century. It is the burial place of King Alfred the Great, King Cnut and King William II, better known as the quick-tempered William Rufus. It is also where Mary Tudor, Henry VIII's eldest child and queen of England from 1553 to 1558, chose to marry Philip of Spain. Given the symbolism of the rose to both church and monarchy, Austin could not have chosen a more fitting salute than this perfect white rose.

Flowering Repeat-flowers; keep deadheading to promote flowering
Aspect Sunny
Soil Rich, moist and well drained
Habit Bushy shrub
Average height 48 in (1.2 m)
Average spread 48 in (1.2 m)
Pruning When established, improve interior architecture and cut back by one-third
Foliage Midgreen
Thorns Yes
As a cut flower An exceptionally fragrant, pure white bloom
Similar varieties Desdemona; Tranquillity

Felicia

Felicia is a charming Parisian corsage of a rose, though it was actually introduced by the esteemed, and very English, Reverend Joseph Hardwick Pemberton (see p. 21), in 1928. He is famous for creating a number of beautiful Hybrid Musks, Felicia included. The parentage results in many of these roses being Floribunda in form – producing great bunches of flowers, with a strong Musk-rose perfume. The sheer abundance of blooms ensures that their fragrance floats in the air.

Felicia's looks belie her upright English roots; she is a ruffled chaos of perfectly pink petals that fade charmingly from a sweet blush pink to a creamy buff, with all shades in between. From pale raspberry buds, she bursts into feminine flower and, like a great courtesan, ages magnificently. Blooms reach around 3 in (8 cm) in diameter and appear in clusters of 5–15 blooms, the clusters increasing in size through the flowering season. But on top of all this beauty, there is Felicia's intoxicating perfume. This is a rose to bury your nose in and inhale with all the strength you can muster.

Felicia is a shrub that responds well to some tender loving care, doing best if fed regularly. It can be left to grow into a generous arching shrub; just give it a light prune or cut it back harder to keep its growth restricted. Be patient and keep feeding; it takes time to reach its full magnificence.

Flowering Repeat-flowers
Aspect Sunny but will tolerate partial shade
Soil Rich, moist and well drained
Habit Shrub
Average height 59 in (1.5 m)
Average spread 59 in (1.5 m)
Pruning Either prune lightly to shape or keep in firm check
Foliage Dark green
Thorns Some
As a cut flower A perfect, fragrant beauty
Similar varieties Leander; Heritage

Duchesse de Brabant

There is a portrait of Marie-Henriette of Austria, later Duchess of Brabant, by Franz Xaver Winterhalter that does not reflect the tragedy of her life after her marriage to the brutish and bullying King Leopold II of Belgium. Like Winterhalter's delicate portrait, the Duchesse de Brabant rose, introduced in 1857 by the French rose grower H. B. Bernède, is an equally fitting tribute to a woman dubbed the "Rose of Brabant" by the people of Belgium. It has all the delicacy and finesse of a Winterhalter portrait.

It is a truly spectacular rose, producing long, shell-pink buds that open into a papery sugar-pink confection – a cup of curling petals. The color is variable and can be more intense – even with a hint of peach – but it always produces a delicious array of washed-sorbet tones. The blooms reach a diameter of around 2¾ in (7 cm). Duchesse de Brabant has a strong Tea-rose perfume that lingers, even when the flower is cut and as it matures. The flowers grow in clusters of 3–5 blooms and nod their heavy heads, releasing perfume into the air. They do not survive rain showers well, so this is a shrub that does best in warmer climates.

It is often stated that Duchesse de Brabant was US president Theodore Roosevelt's favorite rose and that he had a penchant for wearing it as a boutonniere. Sadly, pictures of Roosevelt – something of a dandy, it must be said – reveal a rather more macho approach to his public image; perhaps the Duchesse de Brabant was a private passion. This rose is also known as Comtesse de Labarthe, Comtesse Ouvaroff, Shell and, somewhat unflatteringly, Countess Bertha.

Flowering Repeat-flowers
Aspect Sunny
Soil Rich, moist and well drained
Habit Bushy shrub
Average height 39 in (1 m)
Average spread 39 in (1 m)
Pruning Remove dead and diseased wood in winter and improve the interior architecture
Foliage Midgreen
Thorns Few
As a cut flower Exquisite
Similar varieties Mme. Joseph Schwartz

Rose de Rescht

This is a mysterious rose – its true origin is unknown – but it was brought to England in the 1940s by a Miss Nancy Lindsay, who claims to have found it in an old Persian garden in ancient Rescht [*sic*] – doubtless Rasht in Iran, a flourishing city on the Caspian Sea. Lindsay, a plant collector and daughter of society gardener Norah Lindsay, seems to have been a colorful and somewhat fractious character, however she deserves acknowledgment for rediscovering this deeply fragrant rose.

A bushy shrub, it produces short-stemmed bright pink buds in clusters of 3–7. The double, dark pink flowers are packed with wavy, ruffled petals that turn a lovely purple pink as they mature. Blooms reach a diameter of around 2½ in (6 cm) and you might see a small golden eye at their center. It has a deliciously intense fragrance.

There is some disagreement amongst experts as to whether this is in origin a Gallica, a Damask, a cross between the two, or indeed a Portland.

Flowering Repeat-flowers if deadheaded
Aspect Sunny but will tolerate partial shade
Soil Rich, moist and well drained
Habit Bushy shrub
Average height 39 in (1 m)
Average spread 29 in (75 cm)
Pruning Benefits from a good hard prune every few years
Foliage Pale green
Thorns Yes
As a cut flower Short stemmed but you can float the blooms in bowls or pop them into narrow-necked bottles and keep topping the water off
Similar varieties *Rosa gallica* var. *officinalis* (the Apothecary's rose; see p. 14)

William Lobb

Generally hailed as one of the best Old roses, William Lobb produces bristle-covered dark pink buds. These open to glorious wavy rosettes in shades of dusky pink to intense purple pink, sometimes almost wine colored, with the backs of the petals paler in color. The shades are variable, depending on conditions. The blooms, which reach around 4 in (10 cm) in diameter, age beautifully, fading to lavender as they mature and scattering fragrant petals everywhere. The weight of these multipetaled blooms makes the stems droop. At the base of the petals is a white splash and in the eye there is a small cluster of sulfur-yellow stamens, which darken with age. The flowers have a superb, strong Old-rose scent.

This is a vigorous shrub, which will happily blend with other plants at the back of the border. It can benefit from supports – chestnut coppices work extremely well. It can also be trained as a climber but just bear those thorns in mind. It flowers less well in hot climates.

The French grower Jean Laffay introduced William Lobb in 1855. It is named after the Cornish plant collector who brought the monkey puzzle tree and other conifers to Britain, leading to him being dubbed "the messenger of the big tree." Given the Royal Horticultural Society's Award of Garden Merit in 1993, William Lobb is also known as Duchesse d'Istrie and Old Velvet Moss.

Flowering Once
Aspect Sunny but will tolerate partial shade
Soil Rich, moist and well drained
Habit Tall, vigorous shrub or climber
Average height 98 in (2.5 m)
Average spread 59 in (1.5 m)
Pruning Remove old, dead and diseased wood; deadhead after flowering
Foliage Soft green
Thorns Many
As a cut flower Gorgeous cut flowers but wear gloves to pick
Similar varieties Tour de Malakoff

Coupe d'Hébé

This is a sugar-pink powder puff of a rose, a ruffled petticoat of perfumed petals that form a goblet-shaped bloom. The dark pink buds open to many layers of pleated petals, which twist and fold in the center, modestly concealing the stamens. The flowers reach a diameter of around 3 in (8 cm) and they bloom in clusters of 3–5 buds. The elegant blooms fade and become more papery with age. There is only one flush of flowers, but the weight of the intensely fragrant blooms makes the heads droop and nod and perfume the air. The flowers are followed by red hips.

This rose has a quite upright growth and can be trained as a climber. It is somewhat susceptible to mildew so may require spraying. If you prune it too hard it won't flower.

Coupe d'Hébé was introduced by the French grower Jean Laffay in 1840. The literal translation of the name suggests that it was named in homage to Hebe – Hébé in French – daughter of Zeus and Hera, and cupbearer to the gods. She was supposed to have had the power to give eternal life.

Flowering Once but profusely
Aspect Sunny but will tolerate partial shade
Soil Rich, moist and well drained
Habit Tall shrub or climber
Average height 98 in (2.5 m)
Average spread 59 in (1.5 m)
Pruning Light in late summer
Foliage Bright green and glossy
Thorns Few
As a cut flower Simply stunning and fragrant
Similar varieties Queen of Denmark

Lady Emma Hamilton

The auburn-haired Lady Hamilton was the great beauty of her day. Undoubtedly something of a saucy minx, she made her living by her looks and eventually met and married the considerably older Sir William Hamilton. While living with him in Naples, she met Lord Nelson, who quickly became besotted and eventually abandoned his wife and family for her. After Nelson's death at the Battle of Trafalgar, Emma was left without an income, and after a spell in a debtor's prison, died penniless in Calais.

This rose was introduced by David Austin (see p. 25) in 2005 and named after the beautiful Emma Hamilton to commemorate the 200th anniversary of the Battle of Trafalgar.

It is appropriate that a rose named after Emma should be gloriously flamboyant in hue and intoxicatingly perfumed. It buds dark red with orange flashes and opens into a goblet of incurving, rich gold and tangerine petals. The color is intense, with hints of apricot and a deep sulfur yellow producing warm, glowing blooms that reach around 3 in (8 cm) in diameter. It has a distinctly fruity perfume and has been described by perfumers as having a top note of citrus-fruit zest underpinned by nectarine.

It took the Royal Horticultural Society's Award of Garden Merit in 2012 and was awarded first prize in the 2007 Biennial Fragrant Rose Competition, which is judged by a panel of *grands nez* – leading international perfumers.

Flowering Repeat-flowers
Aspect Sunny
Soil Rich, moist and well drained
Habit Upright, bushy shrub
Average height 48 in (1.2 m)
Average spread 35 in (90 cm)
Pruning Light in summer to encourage repeat-flowering; reduce in winter by one- to two-thirds
Foliage Bronze purple when young, turning dark green
Thorns Yes
As a cut flower Superb, fragrant flowers that will light up any dark corner
Similar varieties The Lady Gardener

Lady Emma
Hamilton

Heritage

Heritage is a rose of delicate beauty, infused with the softest shades of pink and with an absolutely fabulous fragrance. It buds a pale pink, opening to a beautiful cupped bloom with incurving petals. The outer petals are a washed creamy white with the merest hint of pink, grading perfectly to inner petals of an enchanting blush pink. The bush carries masses of flowers from top to toe, especially in the first flush, and these have a strong perfume infused with notes of honey, fruit and carnations. The blooms reach a diameter of around 3½ in (9 cm), occasionally opening widely enough to reveal their stamens.

It litters its petals freely and sheds them within a few days as a cut flower but it is so exquisitely lovely that it is more than worth the effort. The blooms don't much care for the rain, so rush out and collect armfuls of flowers if the weather forecast is bad.

Deadhead to promote repeat-flowering and leave at the end of the season if you want rose hips. This shrub fares better in cooler climates; in hot conditions, the blooms open and shed quickly. It is prone to black spot and benefits from spraying. David Austin (see p. 25) introduced Heritage in 1984.

Flowering Repeat-flowers
Aspect Sunny but will tolerate partial shade
Soil Rich, moist and well drained
Habit Bushy, upright shrub
Average height 48 in (1.2 m)
Average spread 39 in (1 m)
Pruning Reduce by one- to two-thirds in winter
Foliage Glossy dark green
Thorns Few
As a cut flower Exquisite but sheds its petals rather quickly
Similar varieties The Ancient Mariner

Souvenir de la Malmaison

This Old rose can more than hold its own against many of its younger competitors in both looks and perfume. There are numerous stories about the origins of its name but it was probably simply christened in tribute to the Empress Josephine's supposedly superb rose garden at Malmaison (see p. 18). She died in 1814, some 30 years before this rose was introduced.

Souvenir de la Malmaison buds blush pink and initially opens to a pale green pink, then opens further to pale sugar-pink cupped flowers. The petals are quilled and quartered to form technically exquisite and visually perfect blooms that exude a strong Tea-rose fragrance. They reach an impressive diameter of around 5 in (12 cm) and flatten and fade beautifully as they mature to creamy white confections.

This rose can be purchased as a shrub or a climber. It is a slow starter, so you need to be in a position to give it time to grow. Needless to say, any great old lady has a few idiosyncrasies. Souvenir de la Malmaison prefers the warmth– she's a tender soul and does much better in warm climates. The blooms spoil easily in the rain and unopened buds frustratingly rot, ball and brown. Nevertheless, it is still a fabulous rose and was hugely popular with nineteenth-century florists in Lyon.

It was introduced in 1843 by the rose grower Jean Béluze of Lyon, who guarded it jealously, reputedly selling it for an impressive 25 francs in 1845 – a vast sum at that time, which put it out of reach of all but the very wealthy.

Flowering Repeat-flowers
Aspect Sunny and sheltered
Soil Rich, moist and well drained
Habit Spreading shrub or climber
Average height Shrub 39 in (1 m); climber 119 in (3 m)
Average spread 71 in (1.8 m)
Pruning Reduce shrubs by one- to two-thirds in winter
Foliage Glossy midgreen
Thorns Yes
As a cut flower Huge papery blooms, albeit short stemmed, with a strong fragrance
Similar varieties Souvenir de Mme. Auguste Charles

Munstead Wood

This is a sultry, intense rose in a deep, dark red. It has a warm, fruity Old-rose fragrance with notes of blackberry, blueberry and damson. It buds a perfect scarlet, opening to a cupped whorl of pleated and folded petals of a dark burgundy red. The outer petals are lighter in tone, which enhances this bloom's dark heart. As the flowers open still further, you might catch a glimpse of the bright gold stamens. The blooms are held quite erect.

David Austin (see p. 25) introduced this rose in 2007 and named it after the Surrey Arts and Crafts home of garden designer Gertrude Jekyll (see p. 21). The house marked the first of Jekyll's fruitful collaborations with architect Edwin Lutyens. She lived there for 35 years until her death in 1932, and created an extraordinarily beautiful garden there.

Munstead Wood has won several awards, including the Gold Medal for Fragrance at the Japan Rose Society trials in 2011.

Flowering Repeat-flowers
Aspect Sunny but will tolerate partial shade
Soil Rich, moist and well drained
Habit Bushy shrub
Average height 35 in (90 cm)
Average spread 23½ in (60 cm)
Pruning Improve the interior architecture when dormant; deadhead to promote flowering
Foliage Bronze when young, turning midgreen
Thorns Yes
As a cut flower Superb and fragrant
Similar varieties William Shakespeare; Thomas à Becket

Pruning and Care

Ever since humans put pen to paper, they have been dictating how best to grow roses. Millions and millions of words have been written advising how to position, plant, feed, deadhead, prune, not to prune, spray, treat diseases and propagate. The advice is not wrong. However, it can give the false impression that growing roses is a complicated business. Roses are gratifyingly easy to grow – you only have to see how they not only survive in the wild but thrive to realize that these delicate, beautiful flowers do very nicely without any human assistance at all.

If you wanted me to paraphrase rose growing into a single sentence, I'd say: buy one you like the look of, dig a hole, sling it in and give it some water while it settles in. Beyond that, how you care for it is very much your own private business. That's it, pure and simple.

The rigidly upright Hybrid Tea roses that swept to popularity in Queen Victoria's reign and flourished in formal rose gardens, suburban gardens and florist shops the length and breadth of Britain were lovingly nurtured by men who sought to produce outsize, perfectly sculpted blooms. Producing these showy giants required the artful wielding of secateurs (pruning clippers), the calculated destruction of pests and diseases, and regular feeding. In short, it took time and gave the illusion that all rose growing required the same level of tender loving care.

Vintage roses, despite their extravagant, overblown, multipetaled personalities, are far less needy and attention seeking. It is these roses that give me joy. I have planted them in all my gardens and they have rewarded me with a seemingly never-ending supply of fragrant blooms. I make raids on the bushes and arrange the flowers in any old receptacle – jam jars and small bottles are my personal favorites – dot them about the house, take them into work or give out as posies at dinner parties. If nothing else, it gives the illusion that you have a seriously lovely garden.

My cut roses may drip insects (notably earwigs), the leaves may be spotted and the blooms imperfect, but they are still breathtakingly lovely. Almost without exception, they send people into raptures. They are not flowers that can be bought – well, not without spending a small fortune.

My best performing rose bush came with the house, where it loomed large in the front garden. It was a fulsome yellow rose – not my favorite color – and filled me with trepidation. But how wrong can you be? I loved that rose – a Graham Thomas; it flowered without ceasing from late April through to October and I could always find a bud or two for the Christmas Day table. It was an uplifting source of joy from start to finish and I mourned its loss when we moved on.

Opposite Perle d'Or (see p. 57)

How to select your rose

While you can purchase potted roses year-round, the very best and most cost-effective way to buy and plant roses is to purchase them bare rooted between November and April, when they are naturally dormant. Bare-rooted roses get established more quickly and flower in the first year. They do require you to have a little self-discipline but it's a joy when they arrive in the mail at the start of winter, and you plant them and wait for the first flowers in the summer.

There are literally thousands upon thousands of roses to choose from and this is the fun part. Roses can easily be bought online direct from the grower; there are tempting pictures and fulsome descriptions to guide you, and you can choose the perfect rose for your situation. Having said this, I am also prey to the odd impulse buy, and often purchase potted roses from garden retailers – especially when they sell them off cheaply at the end of the season. One of my favorite roses was purchased for a mere £3 because I just couldn't resist this beautiful bargain.

I am also a great fan of trawling gardens for inspiration. Sometimes you see a rose you simply have to have – and if you feel passionately about it, take the trouble to find out its name. Even if it's not labeled, the gardener can often tell you what it is. Buy it for yourself and it will most likely give you years and years of pleasure.

Climate control

Roses grow easily in temperate climates, such as we have in the UK, where the summers are warm and the winters are cold but not frozen.

This is the environment of choice for the rose. But if your climate is more extreme, you may need to be more selective.

In very hot climates, roses can go into shock when the heat hits; blooms can bud, flower and die with terrifying speed. In humid climates, they can suffer from fungal diseases, and when conditions are arid and water is the issue, the soil needs to be kept cool with mulches.

Wild roses grow all over the world but conditions can defeat the less hardy, cultivated types. There are areas of the world where it is simply too frozen, which is why you don't find famous rose gardens in large swathes of Canada, Russia and Greenland, or in places where they need protection from the cold.

Whatever your climate, it is well worth paying attention to which roses thrive in your immediate vicinity; these should be your fail-safe choice. If you want more in-depth advice about rose-hardiness zones, most national rose societies publish guides. In the USA, for instance, there are an impressive 11 zones, ranging from Zone 1, in areas such as Anchorage, where winter temperatures can drop to -51°F (-46°C), to Zone 11 in Hawaii, where the lows never go below 39°F (4°C).

Situation

The long and the short of it is, roses like sunshine and although you can find some varieties that will tolerate shade, they will never do as well as they would if they were basking in the warmth – south-facing sites are best for tender species. Roses also like to be sheltered from strong winds.

The golden rule is never to plant them under trees. I have some in my garden that were planted by my predecessors under a tulip tree and for six months of the year they get almost no sun at all. They flower but not excessively; I am glad that they are there, but they would do a whole lot better in the sun. When it comes to roses I am not of a ruthless disposition, but experts would advise that if a rose isn't performing, you should get rid of it and put something more suitable there instead. But never, ever put a new rose in place of an old one – it simply won't thrive.

If your garden receives partial shade – and most do – remember that roses do better in the morning sun than in the afternoon sun, so plant them where the morning sun strikes. North-facing sites are the trickiest of all.

The perfect bed

Soil is graded according to its clay, silt and sand content. The size and proportion of these mineral particles affect the behavior of the soil. Loam soils have the perfect combination of mineral particles, with about 10–25 percent clay – a mix that offers high fertility with good drainage and good water retention. All soils can be improved with compost, manure and lime.

Roses will grow in almost any soil, though they are much harder work when it is sandy. They also struggle if the soil is not well drained; roses don't appreciate having wet feet. A good, crumbly loam is best. But even if your soil is not ideal, you can work on it to swing the balance. If your ground is a wet and heavy clay, improve the drainage in that area: dig a deep ditch (taking care not to cut through any pipes), put in gravel, top it with a permeable membrane to stop the soil leaching into the gravel, then refill the soil and incorporate masses of manure, compost and some grit.

If your soil is sandy, it will leach moisture and nutrients. Dig it over in late winter and incorporate masses of garden compost, leaf mold and well-rotted manure – roughly 1–2 buckets per square yard (meter). Plant the roses in spring, but even then you will need to water them regularly.

The ideal soil for growing roses has a pH balance of 6.5. Soil pH-testing kits are readily available in shops and garden centers and can tell you the pH of your own particular soil. A pH of 7 indicates a neutral soil, while a reading above 7 means that you have an alkaline soil. It is possible to slightly raise or lower your pH levels: if you add sulfur to the soil it makes it more acid, while the addition of lime will make it more alkaline. But you don't have to do this; I took a reading once, in one of my gardens, but never bothered to do anything with the result – the task was too overwhelming. I just went ahead and planted as best I could, adding wheelbarrow loads of organic matter as I went. Just keep mulching is my rule.

Planting

Having asserted that roses are not attention seekers, it must be stated that they do respond to some tender loving care. If you plant them in well-prepared soil in a well-dug hole – it is best to do so from late autumn to late spring – then top-dress with some well-rotted compost or manure; the worms will do the work for you, carrying the goodness down to the roots. You can then forget about your roses for a year; they'll flower happily and grow encouragingly.

The real secret is to prepare the ground properly. Dig over the spot you plan to use to a depth of about 12 in (30 cm), put in plenty of well-rotted manure and fork it in well. Ideally leave it for a few weeks before you plant. This will give your rose the best start and will provide it with food for many years to come. If you plan on ordering bare-rooted roses, it is easy to organize the preparation in advance, then all the work is done before your roses arrive and planting them out will be a quick and easy affair. You don't want to leave them sitting around waiting; the sooner they can be planted the better.

When you are ready to plant, water the soil well, dig a hole that is wider than it is deep, spread out the roots of your rose, pop it in and gently push the soil back around it. Firm the soil lightly around the rose and water again. Job done. You can now sit back and wait for your first flowers. So little effort for such riches.

Deadheading

I never think about deadheading; I just pick my roses endlessly, which does the job. And if, while you're picking, you snip off any blooms that are finished, you never really have to do any mass deadheading. Later in the year, if your rose produces hips, you can stop deadheading and leave the colorful hips to develop. I was once asked if my rose hips were tomatoes, so plump and round and red were they. The rose in question was a *Rosa rugosa* 'Alba'.

Some of my roses get less of a prune and more of an annual, ruthless deadheading exercise. The purpose of deadheading, aside from aesthetics, is to stop the rose putting energy into the production of hips, leaving it free to produce more flowers.

The thorny issue of pruning

Pruning is much easier than the experts might have you believe. I have attacked roses with an electric trimmer, garden shears, secateurs (pruning clippers) and, I have to confess in the early days, a pair of nail scissors. Without fail they have responded. Don't ever be deterred from growing roses because they might need pruning. You'll learn as you go, and they are very forgiving plants.

Pruning is a job to be undertaken annually, when the rose has finished flowering and stopped growing. In temperate climates, such as we have in the UK, the winters are generally not hard so you can prune any time between December and late March. Since the plant is dormant then, there will be no new shoots to be damaged by frost. Later, spring pruning is advisable in areas where winters are hard; new shoots will burst forth too late for any frost. I often tackle this job in the depths of winter when there is nothing else to be done in the garden and when my thick coat and gloves protect me from the thorns. It is a very therapeutic exercise over the Christmas break. Tidy as you go; remove fallen leaves from around the rose as these will be a source of infection.

THE THREE DS: DEAD, DAMAGED, DISEASED

The basic rule when pruning is to first remove any dead, damaged or diseased wood. All roses benefit from this approach and if you follow this principle you won't go far wrong. A pair of secateurs (pruning clippers) is a small investment and an essential tool for rose growers. They last for years and local hardware shops can sharpen them for you to make the task of pruning easy. Below you'll find a simple guide. I'm not detailing the minutiae of how you prune every single kind of rose. All you need to start you off are the basics, and if you never get beyond these you'll be doing just fine.

Take heart from Vita Sackville-West's advice and "let your roses ramble." She observed that during World War Two, although flower gardens were full of weeds, roses were thriving on benign neglect. Pruning can sometimes be undertaken too enthusiastically; if your rose isn't flowering, feed it, then leave it alone for a few years and see what happens.

After pruning, clear up old leaves and cuttings to help to reduce the spread of disease.

WHERE TO CUT

The basic rule is to cut ¼ in (5 mm) above a bud (new growth, not the flower). Ideally use a good pair of clean, sharp secateurs (pruning clippers). Cut away a little at a time – it will be quite obvious what needs to be removed. And angle the cuts so that rain will run away from the bud.

PRUNING SHRUB ROSES

Remove dead, damaged or diseased wood – you probably won't even need to do this for several years if your rose is new.

Then, as an annual exercise, when they are around three years of age, cut the main shoots back by one-third, and be harder on the side shoots, cutting these back to around 3 in (8 cm).

Improve the interior architecture of the bush by removing any crossing or rubbing branches.

If, over time, your roses start outgrowing their space, you may need to be a little more brutal to keep them at the desired height.

PRUNING CLIMBERS

These are best pruned in winter but you can cut back the long young stems or tie them into place in autumn to avoid them being damaged by winter winds. Begin by removing dead, diseased or damaged branches. Old, unproductive stems should be removed low on the plant. Tie in new growth to fill any gaps and cut back the side shoots to around 3 in (8 cm). Vita Sackville-West revealed that she never pruned her roses at Sissinghurst. She went on to explain that she did, however, remove dead and dying wood, but rather than prune, she tied in new growth to the wall, bending it this way and that to encourage the plant to produce new shoots along its length.

PRUNING RAMBLERS

These once-flowering roses can be left to do their own thing and they'll scramble over all manner of unsightly objects, providing a superb screen. But they are very undisciplined and you will need to give them a hard prune here and there if they start to reach monstrous proportions. If you are growing a rambler over an arch or pergola, treat it like a climber in terms of training and pruning.

Maintenance feeds

When you've finished pruning, it's time to think about giving your rose some food to help it grow well and flower plentifully. Repeat-flowerers are especially greedy; they need the nutrients to help them generate that mass of blooms. Because I am lazy, I tend to throw a shovelful of horse manure around the base of my roses – but then I have horses passing by daily so it feels wasteful not to utilize their deposits. Fresh, steaming manure isn't good for the plant though; you must give it time to age first. If it's stopped smelling, it's probably ready. The worms will carry the goodness down into the soil. The manure also helps to keep the soil cool and helps water retention. Alternatively, you might find it easier to feed with a slow-release fertilizer, available in all good garden centers, after which, add a good mulch of compost or well-rotted manure to help keep the soil cool and the water in.

Once you're into the flowering season, you can apply a fertilizer that is high in nitrogen to promote flower production, but only do this at the tail end of a flush of flowering in order to promote the next spate of flowers.

Pests and diseases

As I am not hellbent on perfection in my roses, I have rarely had cause to spray, the one exception being a terrible case of powdery mildew that blighted my green-eyed Madame Hardy. It was not such a problem except it tended to spread to other roses in the vicinity, so I braced myself to wield the spray gun, which is something I prefer not to do.

Dear reader, I confess that after a couple of years of spraying, I put Madame out of her misery. It was my fault not hers; she is a lovely rose and I was a mere callow youth, who had blithely ignored all the planting instructions regarding aspect. So take note: please follow planting instructions. Below is a list of some of the most common rose pests and diseases so that you can tackle problems if they occur.

POWDERY MILDEW

The fungus *Podosphaera pannosa* coats shoots, leaves, young stems and flower stalks with a fine white powder, as the name of the disease indicates. Infuriatingly, it can prevent the buds from opening. The cause is often high humidity combined with a dry soil and poor airflow. By giving the plant a good mulch you'll help improve the soil condition and at the same time inhibit water loss. Water any affected roses regularly in dry spells, ruthlessly prune out all infected leaves and shoots, and clear them away to help prevent reinfection.

You can also use chemical controls – fungicides that will often help against some of the other common rose complaints. Spray regularly through the growing season and again in late summer and early autumn to help prevent the fungus overwintering in the dormant buds. You want to break the cycle, if possible. Some varieties of rose are more susceptible to powdery mildew than others.

BLACK SPOT

The fungal infection *Diplocarpon rosae* is self-evident when it appears – the rose leaves are peppered with black spots, like pirates on a murderous mission. The spores germinate in warm weather if the leaves have been wet for seven hours plus. If watering your roses, try to do so in the morning, when the leaves stand a better chance of drying quickly. Some varieties of rose are more susceptible to this fungal infection, but even in disease-resistant roses the fungus can develop new strains and blight them. As usual, good housekeeping can help inhibit the spread of black spot – always clear up dropped leaves from around the base of the plant in autumn.

RUST

This is a dastardly menace when it occurs. The spores of *Phragmidium* are spread on the wind, so can strike the plant at any time. The first signs are orange speckling, then orange spots, on both sides of the leaves. The leaves will drop as they become increasingly affected and the spores will overwinter, ready to reinfect the plant the following spring.

Look out for black pustules appearing on the leaves in late summer; this is another warning sign. Cut out any affected stems, clear up fallen leaves to help prevent reinfection and destroy them – don't put them on the compost heap. Prune the rose so that its interior architecture is airy and open. If you are not averse to chemical treatments, spray thoroughly with a copper fungicide in the spring. Some Old-rose varieties are much more susceptible to rust.

APHIDS

If you grow roses, somewhere along the line you'll get sap-sucking aphids – they come in green, pink and white varieties. They cluster on flower buds, shoots and leaves, and excrete honeydew, which encourages the growth of the sooty mold that looks just like it sounds. If you spot ants on your rose, they are another indicator that there are lots of aphids around. Ants love honeydew and have a symbiotic relationship with aphids, herding and caring for them to obtain the honeydew.

Aphids don't damage the plant as such but they can distort flower buds, and can make the plant something of an unsightly mess. If you spot them early, you can pick them off and squash between your fingers, or you can spray them; there are nonbiological sprays that are effective, though you have to be diligent. If ants are in evidence, deter them by putting sticky bands around the rose stems or by treating the ants' nest with a chemical control. This leaves the aphids more vulnerable to predators and prevents the ants from relocating the aphids.

ROSES IN THE HOUSE

Ungrateful wretch that I am, I simply loathe being given bunches of roses. As I have stated elsewhere, the vast majority of florists' roses are gaudily colored, devoid of fragrance, suffer from drooping heads and, to add the final insult, the flowers never fully open. As far as I am concerned, they are not merely a poor substitute for a garden rose but an absolute travesty.

Garden roses will give you no such problems and almost nothing in this world is more beautiful. I am no Martha Stewart when it comes to flower arrangements – a lone rose in a tiny bottle or some jam jars filled with stems of roses dotted around the house make me very happy indeed. A sprig or two of lavender, catmint, honeysuckle, Lady's mantle or rosemary merely enhances the effect. Roses are so exquisite that this simple approach often serves to underline their natural beauty.

There's certainly no need for expensive vases. In describing roses as cut flowers, please remember that short-stemmed garden roses are less suited to stiff, formal arrangement – and are all the lovelier for it.

A chaotic mix of colors is incredibly pretty – pinks, creams, whites and even coppery yellows will blend prettily together. Red and dark purple roses are the exception to this rule; these look so spectacular with blue or lavender flowers that I cannot bear to arrange them with anything else, but that is a personal idiosyncrasy.

To get the very best from your garden roses, cut them early in the morning and use a sharp pair of scissors or secateurs (pruning clippers) – you don't want to compress the stem when you cut, which will restrict the uptake of water. Ideally you'll have a container of water handy to pop them straight into – though I confess I rarely bother. Once in the house, strip off all the lower leaves, while keeping the rose in water. Cut the stem to the desired length, again keeping it immersed in water, and pop it straight into your clean vase (use a little bleach whenever you empty a vase to get rid of any bacteria and clean it thoroughly).

Vases should be full of tepid water. Change the water every couple of days and trim a little more off the stems to ensure that the uptake of water remains good. Try to place your vase out of direct sunlight.

Finally, make it a rule that you will always have at least one rose in any old container beside the kitchen sink.

Enjoy!

GLOSSARY

Anther: The pollen-producing part of the plant, which rests atop the filament; together they make up the stamen.

Balling: Referring to a flower that does not open but instead rots while in bud.

Bare rooted: Sold without its roots in soil.

Bush rose: A rose that requires close pruning (see below) annually.

Calyx: The green protective cover of the bud; opens into five sepals.

Climber: A rose that will grow up to a good height; it needs support.

Close prune: A formal annual prune that cuts the rose back to at least one-third of its height.

Cultivar: A cultivated variety that has been produced by selective breeding.

Deadheading: Snipping off dead flowers from the plant.

Double: Used loosely, a flower that has numerous rows of petals; technically a flower with 20–40 petals.

Filament: The leggy stem that supports the anther; together they make up the stamen.

Floribunda: A rose bearing dense clusters of flowers.

Fully double: A flower that has over 40 petals.

Group: Cultivars that have similar characteristics.

Hips: The fruit of the rose.

Hybrid: The crossing of different species or varieties.

Modern Garden roses: Roses established after 1867, when the development of La France marked the birth of the Hybrid Tea, crossing Tea roses and Hybrid Perpetuals. Modern Garden roses are propagated asexually. Confusingly, many Modern Garden roses have Old Garden roses in their ancestry. Classifications include the Floribunda, Hybrid Tea, Grandiflora, Miniature and Polyantha.

Old Garden roses: Roses established before 1867 and propagated asexually. Classifications include Alba, Ayrshire, Bourbon, Centifolia or Provence, China, Damask, Gallica, Hybrid Perpetual, Hybrid Rugosa, Hybrid Sempervirens, Moss, Noisette, Portland and Tea roses.

Pistil: The flower's female reproductive parts.

Pompom: Like its rounded woolly namesake, a rounded bloom with short, regular petals.

Quartered: A flower that produces petals that are folded into sections.

Quilled: A petal curled into the shape of a quill.

Rambler: A vigorous rose that will scramble and climb; has long, flexible whips (see below).

Semidouble: A flower that has 10–20 petals.

Sepal: The five green parts of the calyx that enclose the flower in tight bud, reflexing to reveal the petals.

Shrub rose: A rose that is allowed to grow in its natural form and requires only less rigorous pruning.

Single: A rose that has fewer than 10 petals and usually five.

Species: Wild plants that reproduce naturally.

Sport: A change in the genetic makeup of a plant, often causing changes in color or form.

Stamen: The flower's male reproductive parts, made up of the filament and the anther.

Sucker: An undesirable shoot from the rootstock.

Variety: In roses, this term refers to a cultivated rose with heritable characteristics.

Whip: A slender unbranched shoot.

Wild roses: Often also called Species roses, these are the wild plants that reproduce naturally.

x: Indicates a hybrid in a plant's name.

INDEX

Jane's Acknowledgments

Over the years I have read widely on the subject of roses and I pay humble tribute to the knowledge and skills of these authors – old and new. Their love and passion for their subject inspired and educated me, and I beg their indulgence for all too frequently ignoring their words of wisdom when it came to cultivating my own roses. I also ask their forgiveness for callously disregarding the use of formal classifications and for wantonly playing fast and loose with the accepted color terminology; I am more colorist than rosarian.

I must pay tribute to photographer Georgianna Lane, whose exceptional eye has captured the charm and beauty of these exquisite flowers. She has flown around the world in her efforts to capture the perfect bloom, and without her this book would be nothing.

I have had assistance from more people than I can name, and without their patience and kindness in answering innumerable queries, this book would not have come to fruition.

However, I must single out Michael Marriott, senior rosarian for David Austin Roses, and Mako Hiraoka, technical specialist at David Austin Roses in Japan, without whose expertise I would have been lost.

My daughter Florence kindly found time to spare to proofread my first draft, and my husband, Eric Musgrave, brought me endless cups of tea and patiently listened while I wittered on about this, that and the other rose. My son Teddy and stepdaughter Genevieve provided endless encouragement, and all of my family have kindly tolerated much benign neglect. I must also acknowledge the patience of my friends Aaron Ogles and Gilly Cubitt, who quietly encouraged me to crack on with the work.

At Pavilion I must thank my editors Krissy Mallett and Hilary Mandleberg for their gentle encouragement, forbearance and enthusiasm, Zoë Anspach for her elegant design and Polly Powell for her faith in me.

Intellectual Property Rights – David Austin® Roses

Throughout this book each David Austin® rose variety is referred to by its commercial name (e.g., Heritage™). The variety denomination in relation to worldwide Plant Variety Rights (e.g., Ausblush) and any trademark around the world relating to the commercial name has been omitted for ease of reading. The list below gives variety denominations and the trademark status of the commercial names.

For a definitive list of specific trademark rights for a particular country contact the Licensing Department, David Austin Roses Limited, at +44 1902 376314.

A Shropshire Lad™ (Ausled); Abraham Darby™ (Auscot); Alan Titchmarsh™ (aka Huntington Rose) (Ausjive); Anne Boleyn (Ausecret); Boscobel™ (Auscousin); Brother Cadfael™ (Ausglobe); Buttercup (Ausband); Constance Spry (Ausfirst); Crocus Rose (aka Emanuel™) (Ausquest); Crown Princess Margareta™ (Auswinter); Darcey Bussell™ (Ausdecorum); Desdemona™ (Auskindling);

Georgianna's Acknowledgments

The magnificent roses featured in this book were photographed in a wonderful array of gardens, grand and small, from England and Europe to South America and numerous locations in the United States, including my own Pacific Northwest garden, where I have grown and photographed roses for nearly 10 years.

I am greatly indebted and very grateful to the following individuals and organizations for their truly invaluable assistance, advice and support in the creation of these images.

Author Jane Eastoe has been such a cheerful and positive presence throughout and her delightful writing brings the fascinating history, beauty and grace of these roses to life.

David C. H. Austin, OBE, founder and breeder of David Austin Roses, has exerted a defining influence and Mr. Michael Marriott, senior rosarian for David Austin Roses, provided vital information, guidance and exceptionally generous access to the entire center, including the most magnificent rose fields imaginable.

Author/photographer and well-known rosarian Carolyn Parker welcomed me to her home, her lush garden and her studio, providing her expertise as well as the missing subjects for a number of Old-rose varieties.

María Cecilia Lorca Mateluna, rose lover extraordinaire, shared with me her breathtaking rose garden and magical home of soaring timber and stone in the Andean foothills outside Santiago, Chile.

Dawn Severin, passionate rose grower and owner of All My Thyme Farm in Washington, and her daughter Claire, supplied me with abundant buckets of gorgeous roses as well as creative collaboration while shooting.

My husband and fellow photographer, David Phillips, and my dear family, have been unwavering in their support of this project and my sudden mad dashes across the globe, chasing just one more rose that might be blooming, however briefly, in a far-off land.

And lastly, my very sincere gratitude to Pavilion Books, especially publisher Polly Powell, for envisioning this book and discovering my work, and publishing director Katie Cowan for her guidance and enthusiasm. Senior editor Krissy Mallett has been a bright beacon of encouragement and sanity, while designer Zoë Anspach did the impossible by brilliantly wrangling my overabundance of images into the classical and elegant presentation you see here.

Eglantyne™ (Ausmak); Fighting Temeraire™ (Austrava); Gentle Hermione™ (Ausrumba); Gertrude Jekyll™ (Ausbord); Golden Celebration™ (Ausgold); Grace™ (Auskeppy); Graham Thomas™ (Ausmas); Heritage™ (Ausblush); James Galway™ (Auscrystal); Jubilee Celebration™ (Aushunter); Kathryn Morley™ (Ausclub); Lady Emma Hamilton™ (Ausbrother); Lady of Shalott™ (Ausnyson); Leander™ (Auslea); Lichfield Angel™ (Ausrelate); Mary Rose™ (Ausmary); Morning Mist (Ausfire); Munstead Wood™ (Ausbernard); Olivia Rose Austin™ (Ausmixture); Princess Alexandra of Kent™ (Ausmerchant); Princess Anne™ (Auskitchen); Queen of Sweden (aka Christina™) (Austiger); Scepter'd Isle™ (Ausland); St. Cecilia™ (Ausmit); St. Swithun™ (Auswith); Strawberry Hill™ (Ausrimini); Tam O'Shanter™ (Auscerise); The Alnwick™ Rose (Ausgrab); The Ancient Mariner™ (Ausoutcry); The Generous Gardener™ (Ausdrawn); The Lady Gardener™ (Ausbrass); The Lady's Blush (Ausoscar); Thomas à Becket™ (Auswinston); Tradescant™ (Ausdir); Tranquillity™ (Ausnoble); William Shakespeare™ 2000 (Ausromeo); Winchester Cathedral™ (Auscat)

First published in the United Kingdom in 2016 by
Pavilion, 1 Gower Street, London, WC1E 6HD

Published in the United States of America by
Gibbs Smith
PO Box 667
Layton, Utah 84041

1.800.835.4993 orders
www.gibbs-smith.com

ISBN 978-1-4236-4671-6
Library of Congress Control Number: 2016945731

Printed and bound in China
21 20   5 4